I MASTERED FAILURE BUT LOOK AT ME NOW!

I MASTERED FAILURE BUT LOOK AT ME NOW!

Success Strategies from Those
Who Refused to Stay Down

Wimbrey Training Systems

I MASTERED FAILURE BUT LOOK AT ME NOW!

Success Strategies from Those Who Refused to Stay Down

© 2013 Wimbrey Training Systems

Manufactured in the United States of America

For information, please contact:

Wimbrey Training Systems
205 Edinburgh Court
Southlake, TX 76092

www.JohnnyWimbrey.com

info@JohnnyWimbrey.com

ISBN-13: 978-1-938620-04-1

2013 1 2 3 4 5

Table of Contents

Foreword

It has been said that the richest plots of land in the world aren't the diamond mines in South Africa, nor the oil fields in the Middle East, but rather the graveyards and cemeteries because that's where people and their dreams are buried. There are life-changing and world-changing people and ideas which will never be heard because they never had the chance to reach the masses.

Using their life experiences, these authors have proven that if you have a willingness to do whatever is required, and take the initiative to pursue your dreams, you can make some incredible things happen.

If you are willing to elevate your life beyond your circumstances and allow that to become your life mission, coupled with a strong belief in yourself and in a power greater than yourself, the possibilities of reinventing your life and transforming who you are now into who you can become are unlimited.

This book is designed to empower you with the secret process of success used by those who not only talk the talk, but also more importantly, walk the walk.

You will go through step-by-step proven methods to transform your life and experience the health, wealth, and happiness we all want. I found every chapter inspiring and enlightening, as I'm sure you will.

These people have accomplished many tremendous things in their lives, and they are sharing the things that they have learned along the way with you. Read it with an open mind and an open heart.

This book will change your life; I guarantee it.

—Les Brown
Motivational Speaker and Author

Chapter 1

Your Past Does Not Equal Your Future!

BY JOHNNY WIMBREY

"Where you've been has nothing to do with where you're going."
- Anonymous

Great athletes prepare for competition through very intense trainings. They experience pain, sweat, and sometimes even tears, but their drive for success and the end results feed the desire to press on. They understand that by lifting weights and exercising they may have pain, sometimes injuries, setbacks, and difficulties, but they also understand they are in the development and maturing process that will get their bodies and minds prepared for competition.

Likewise, I have experienced the weights of life and have been in mentally and emotionally rigorous workouts for years. But you know what? I am personally thankful for every hardship, every trial, and every burden. These personal experiences have molded me to become the well-accomplished, relentless, and victorious man that I am today. I wouldn't change any of the experiences in my life for the world. Just as a champion's workout is more intense than the average, so was mine. I am a champion, and it's because of my emotional and mental growth from my life's weights that I am here today. The best way out of difficulty is through it.

One of my earliest memories in life was living as a child in a battered women's shelter. You always hear that the first impression is the most important. It's true! Like it or not, we are ultimately labeled or prejudged by others' first impressions. It kind of seems unfair, doesn't it?

Well, think about it. Pause right now and take a second to remember someone you met for the first time who really impressed you. I mean, as soon as you saw this person, you immediately knew that he or she had life at its best. When they walked into a room, it lit up. I mean, they had it going on! Now, I want you to think about how you felt in the very moment you saw the person who really impressed you. Did you feel alive, motivated, and energetic?

Now, go to the complete opposite and think of someone you met for the first time who really didn't impress you AT ALL. I mean, this person to your mind was a pitiful sight. When they came into your presence, the whole atmosphere changed for the worse. You may not even have known this person, but somehow, immediately it was obvious that he or she had issues.

Now, think about this person who didn't impress you at all. What did that feel like? Did this person make you feel down, negative, or drained? Did he or she affect your mood, even if it was only temporarily?

The impression in meeting a person for the first time has so much power or impact that it affects the way you immediately characterize a person. It also has the ability to control your mind-set, your ability to think or feel good or bad about them. What about the impact of the first impression of LIFE?

Life Is Not Fair!

Life sucks! I think that would be a fair first impression of my life. When I was three years old, my mother ran for her life with my two older brothers and me. I mean, we literally ran out of our house in Fort Worth, Texas, with no shoes on and no destination.

The government shipped us to San Jose, California, and put us up in a battered woman's shelter without my father having any knowledge of our whereabouts. It did not take me long to figure out that something was wrong with my life.

"Why do we have to put powder and water together to make milk? I see everyone else pouring store-bought milk from a gallon jug."

"Why do we have to eat on the kitchen floor when everyone else eats at the kitchen table?"

"Why does our money come in a booklet, and all the bills are different colors? Everyone else has green money and they aren't limited as to what they can buy. All we can buy with our funny colored money is food."

I was in the first grade and we were just beginning to experience a sense of stability in our lives when my mother decided to pack us up and move back to Texas. I was introduced to my dad, who was a stranger to me at the time. My mother and father never got back together, but because of my mother's financial problems at the time, my brothers and I were forced to live with my father.

After several months of getting settled in and becoming comfortable with our situation, my mother picked us up, for what was supposed to be a short weekend, and took us back to California without my father's knowledge.

I'd just finished the second grade when my mother told us that we would have to go back to Texas to live with our father, but this time she could not come with us. There are no words that can describe the fear and emotions that we went through. She told us not to worry because she would be coming after us shortly.

We did not see our mother again until two years after that. There were months that went by that I thought my mother was dead. When we got back to Texas I was forced to repeat the second grade, and start all over, while living with a man I hardly knew.

"Life is not fair!" That could have been my attitude. Maybe it's yours too. Can I ask you a question? Whoever told you that life was going to be fair?

This is the trap: we believe that life is dealt to us like a hand of cards, and whatever you get is what you get.

Well, I have some breaking news for you. In reality, ladies and gentlemen, you are in complete control of who you are, where you're going, and where you end up. Your destiny is whatever you say it is. It is wherever you see yourself going. If you don't see it or say it, there is no vision, and where there is no vision, people perish. You are and will be whatever you say you are.

In other words, where you come from does not necessarily mean that's where you will end up. A mentor of mine named Dan Mikals once told me, "At some point in your life you must flip the switch." What he was referring to was that until you yourself take action and flip the switch, there will be no change.

It took me many years to realize this fact. For example, all my life people always told me I was very talented and that if I did not use my gifts it would be a waste. I was constantly in trouble as a youth, in school and many other places. My teachers always told me people would kill to have the talents I had.

My problem was I thought they were flat-out lying. I thought that's what they had to say. As if they were paid to flatter us. This used to really piss me off! I was tired of everyone telling me how talented I was and how I was a waste. I mean, they didn't know what I had been through. Although I was in elementary and then junior high, at that time in my life I couldn't slow down enough to think about talents. I was just trying to survive the drugs, alcohol, deadly violence, and whatever else I had to go home to.

Could my teachers relate to a father jamming a gun in their faces, threatening to kill them, or wondering if their mother is alive because they haven't seen her in two years or heard from her in months? I did not want to talk about talents! I wanted to survive! How could anyone see such big talents in someone so small and yet hiding so much pain? How could they ever realize what talents I had?

The reason I got so angry is that they saw something in me I didn't even see in myself. It really hurts when you don't see "it" in yourself. My "it" was success—the talent to believe there was a chance that I, Johnny Wimbrey, could become great! I never thought about the future; all I thought about was what I had to go home to.

Destiny is not a matter of chance, it is a matter of choice; it is not a thing to be waited for, it is a thing to be achieved.

The Moment I Chose to Live

It was Sunday evening, January 31, 1993. I had just turned eighteen a couple days before, and I was watching Super Bowl XXVII's halftime show. The phone rang and I answered it. It was one of my friends, calling to let me know that one of our homies from the hood was shot and killed the night before, at a local bowling alley. Although I had had friends before who were murdered, when I got this message I went numb.

Not only was I good friends with the dead man, I also grew up with the person who killed him. These two individuals represented two different groups in our area. We all went to school together, and we had all been fighting each other since the seventh grade.

In my mind, the real war had just begun. I was very angry and had every intention of retaliating for my friend's murder, but the gang all agreed to wait until after his funeral.

God works in mysterious ways! Friday, February 5, was the night of the wake. We all brought our guns to the church, prepared for anything. Then the victim's mother found the strength somehow to make her way to the microphone and speak to us. We were unprepared for what she had to say.

She began to tell us the story of a recent conversation she had had with her son. She said that Chris, "Mookie," had come to her a few weeks before, and told her he was tired of running, that he was ready to live right. He then had given his mother his gun because he was serious this time.

None of us knew about this incident, but looking back, we realized there had been something different about Mookie lately. When I saw the tears in his mother's eyes, and all the pain she was going through, I was further amazed then to hear her express her forgiveness to the young man who had killed her son.

I had a mental epiphany! Who was I to seek revenge for a friend who had been murdered if his own mother had already found forgiveness?

That night I gave my gun to the preacher. I told him I didn't want to live like that anymore, and I asked for help. I remember praying that night for God to send someone into my life who would help me stay focused on doing what was right. I needed a reason not to go back to the streets.

The very next day, Saturday, February 6, at the age of eighteen, I met the young lady who would several years later become my wife. I remember thinking to myself that this girl is too innocent for me, and I was nowhere near her type. But we were both immediately attracted to each other and became really good friends in a very short period of time. She lived in a middle-class area and had a very loving family.

I remember wanting to impress her and at the same time protect her from my past, present, and potential future. So I began to act, talk, and dress differently around her. We never went to my side of town because I was afraid of the possibilities of her getting caught up in a dangerous situation.

As time went on I remember beginning to think in a way I have never thought before. I began to wonder about my future. Where was I headed, and what could I offer this young lady if our relationship got serious? I valued our relationship so much that I began to change my lifestyle. She gave me a reason and a purpose for wanting more out of life.

Up to that point, I had no idea what possibilities even existed. I was afraid. I had never thought about the future; I lived one day at a time.

Then, I gradually began to think about the future—my future. What did it have in store for me? Immediately, I began to sweat; my heart raced; I was covered in fear.

Thoughts of settling down and the possibilities of ever starting a family of my own terrified me. I did not want my future children's first impression of life to be that of a struggle like mine was. I had a change of attitude, and like Dan Mikals had said, "You must flip the switch," so . . . I flipped the switch!

I was determined to be successful. I didn't care about my past anymore. I had a new attitude, and I was not going to let anyone or anything stand in my way. And the first person I had to get out of my way was me!

Once I made up my mind that success was a "must" and failure was not an option, things began to change: By the time I was twenty, I was self-employed; I became a temporary licensed independent insurance agent. With hard work and determination, within six months I was one of the top agents in the nation with a national health insurance agency. At twenty-two I was having my first house built from the ground up. It was a two-story, four-bedroom home.

Within one month of closing on my new home, on July 27, 1998, I married my high school sweetheart. I then paid off ALL her debt and put her through her last year of college. I told her from day one she would always have the option to work or not work. Needless to say, she has never clocked in for anyone, and she has been the vice president of our home ever since.

My goal for 2000 was to make a six-figure salary by the end of the year. By the end of May, I had earned over $100,000. I was five-and-a-half months ahead of schedule. I was interviewed on national radio stations and a popular television network as a young success story. Since then, I have conducted seminars around the nation, inspiring thousands and empowering the masses for greatness.

I don't say any of this to impress you, but to impress upon you—if I can do it, anyone can! Who would have ever thought that a biracial, young punk ex-drug dealer who could roll a perfect joint by the time he was eight years old, whose earliest memory of life was marked by living in a battered women's shelter because his father was an abusive drunk, could ever gain the attention of tens of thousands of people from all walks of life and inspire them to greatness?

Why would someone listen to me? I don't have a college degree or some prestigious background that would qualify me to speak before thousands. I asked myself this question hundreds of times until I was becoming my own worst enemy. Then, one day, I read a quote that to this day has changed my life forever: "Adversity causes some men to break, others to break records." I began to say it to myself, and I still do every day, adding another sentence. "Adversity causes some men to break; others to break records. And I am a record breaker." As soon as I started to say that to myself, I began to break records. Are you a record breaker? Do you want to be?

What I tell myself may seem a little arrogant, but if you believe that, you are your own greatest enemy. There is nothing wrong with confidence. "Those who don't understand the difference between arrogance and confidence will always be intimidated by confident people." The fact is, if you don't believe in your own greatness, no one else will. How else can you be great unless you believe that you are? And how else can you believe you are unless you're confident in what or who you say you are?

I once heard someone say, "The best way to predict your future is to create one." I'm living proof that this statement is true.

God doesn't make mistakes; we do. The question is not have you made mistakes? The question is will you get back up? Your past does not equal your future. In spite of your past, there are still possibilities. Where you've been has nothing to do with where you're going! The reason they call it the past is because it's behind you. And although your past has everything to do with who you are today, it's not necessary to consult your past to determine your future.

I will go back to where I came from, but only to pull others out.

"The best way to predict your future is to create one." What are you creating for your future? Take control! You are a record breaker!

About Johnny Wimbrey

Internationally acclaimed talk show host, author, and motivational-speaking giant Johnny Wimbrey lives by one rule: Don't let your past determine your future. Living a real-life "G to Gent" story, Wimbrey continues to inspire and change the lives of corporate execs and inner-city kids alike.

After enduring a challenging road and some dispiriting experiences, Johnny managed to dramatically turn his life around and has become one of the most inspirational speakers of our time. Growing up in Fort Worth, Texas, and dealing with the split of his parents at a young age, Johnny learned early on that the only person one can truly rely on is oneself. Forced to fend for himself, he looked to the streets and began an involvement with drugs and gangs. The murder of a close friend served as an eye-opener to Johnny and made him decide that it was finally time to "flip the switch."

With a fresh new outlook and his mind set on success, Johnny set out to reinvent himself, only to learn that significant change did not come easy. Having come from a past with more hardship than opportunity, he found that finding a new career would be a challenge. However, Johnny's determination to succeed surmounted the struggle, and he soon landed a successful career in insurance and credits. His new career gave him a stability that he had never experienced, and more importantly, was a product of his own hard work and genius.

Johnny continued to excel in the insurance business and began spreading his knowledge to new recruits. It was during this time that he realized that he had a remarkable capacity to speak. After much pursuit he began launching his seminars in 2000, which focus on discovering the psychology of success and the traits of a winning mind-set. Since then, Johnny's goal has been to inspire others with the success secrets that his own life has proven to work. In the last year, Johnny has spread his life-enhancing words to audiences around the world, speaking in London, Australia, Singapore, South Africa, Amsterdam, Israel, The Virgin Islands—a list that continues to grow. Johnny has travelled over 170 thousand miles internationally to speak!

In addition to speaking Johnny has written the best-selling book, *From the Hood to Doing Good*, an inspirational work that motivates people to put past pains behind them. Johnny's work has inspired people with a wide variety of struggles to make the positive decisions that have led them to significant life changes. In addition to his book, Johnny has co-authored *Multiple Streams of Inspiration* and *Conversations on Success*, both of which inspire greatness. Johnny also anchors a powerful DVD collection called *Think and Win Big*, which offers mental strategies and gives profound insight into the kind of wisdom needed for success. Johnny recently launched a new magazine entitled *Success University*, which highlights inspirational stories to motivate people.

When not out spreading world-shaking words of wisdom, Johnny is a loving father who enjoys spending time with his family, riding his Harley, and like any true Texan, watching football.

For more information please visit www.johnnywimbrey.com.

Chapter 2

He Lost It All to Lose It All

BY JONATHAN GILLARDI

"Adversity causes some people to break and other people to break records."

- Johnny Wimbrey

I thought I had failure mastered at a young age, and that I'd never be bothered by it again. Boy, was I wrong; or maybe I was just young, naïve and stupid—but either way I was wrong. I'd grown up in a "regular" American middle-class family. Not rich by any means, but not poor either. At least that's what I thought for years. But sometime in my late teens I discovered that my family enjoyed its middle-class lifestyle only because of the fact that both sets of grandparents helped us make ends meet every month. I guess that's part of the reason that I left home after high school and got married, with no real plan of action except to "become a major success someday"—at something.

I was fortunate, though, to land a job at The Prudential before I turned 20. I even received an award as the youngest sales manager ever promoted in Prudential's long history. I also lost more than 500 pounds and conquered obesity, which I had dealt with since my youth. In fact, at my heaviest, I was considered "super super obese" and was almost completely incapacitated.

So by age 25, I honestly thought I'd already mastered failure. All I could see in front of me was great success. But I was about to get a huge wake-up call. In fact "wake-up call" is probably putting it mildly.

Imagine waking up one summer morning in your Plano, Texas, mansion to discover that it wasn't just a few hours after you'd fallen asleep, but rather two *weeks* later—and you were on the floor having just come out of a binge-drinking blackout. Well, that was me. Now, admittedly, I had a huge ego. I thought I must have been having a nightmare, like in the movies. But this was reality, and everything I had and everyone I loved was gone that day in 2002. My wife, my son, my family and my so-called friends. I'd taken it all for granted, everyone and everything. In my crazy mind, I thought *they* were wrong. I really wondered, what had I done to deserve this? Didn't they know I was the "Great and Powerful Jonathan Gillardi"? Obviously, I still had a lot to learn.

As a bit of background, my wife and I and our young son moved to Texas from New York in 2000. I was at the top back then, or so I thought. I'd been very successful in some Internet businesses, and I had the house, the cars, the money, and all the toys any man could ever want. But I had a little secret. During the day I acted like a normal family man—I was "dad," and went to all the little league and pee wee football games, family dinners and barbecues. But at night, I was a vampire rock star: I went partying, clubbing and experimented with party drugs till the wee hours. I would get home just before sunrise, as my son was waking up to get ready for school. I pulled this off for several years and thought life was grand. I had it all; I had my cake and was eating it too.

But my drinking increased. Within six months, I was drinking two big 1.5 liter bottles of tequila a day and was a full-fledged alcoholic. Nothing mattered except alcohol. During the last six months before my wife took off with my son, I drank all day until I passed out. Wherever I went, I went there drunk—to my son's games, dinners, school functions, you name it. And I wasn't a nice drunk, either. I've since heard hundreds of stories about how out of control I was. But somehow, at the time, I really thought everything was perfect.

One memory that I'm sure will always haunt me is when my wife and I were watching our son be interviewed for a school reading program. Of course I was drunk, but I remember my son being asked what he wanted to be when he grew up. His response still floors me today. He replied, "I want to own Internet companies and do all the things my dad does." Wow. Even now it still stings. I was so good at hiding my secret life, even from my little "mini me."

By the time I woke up from that binge-drinking blackout, though, everything was gone. I was completely alone. I was forced to sign over my parental rights and lost my son—who was my whole life—forever. I was such a menace, in fact, that my own brother showed up in court to testify against me. He even told me that I no longer had a brother, which is still the situation today.

Over the next two years, I basically became Howard Hughes. I locked myself away and drank anytime I was awake. I simply didn't care about anything. Most people thought I was either out of the country or dead. Once I came out of seclusion, I tried to get back into society but avoided my old friends. I continued to drink and tried to function, but that led to many problems I'm not proud of. I had relationships with women I shouldn't have been around. I was arrested for public intoxication more than 35 times—twice in the same day on one memorable occasion. I had several DUI charges, spent a total of 14 months in the county jail, had countless other legal problems—oh, and I was homeless. Not knowing how to handle homelessness, I started going to rehab centers just to get off the streets. But once I was released, I'd go back to my old tricks again. I was trying to get back to what I had once known, but it wasn't working.

Finally after a very bad seven months in 2007, I moved to Montana to get away from Texas. But I changed only addresses, not my behavior. Actually, my behavior got worse, if you can believe that.

The grass always seemed to be greener somewhere else, so I left Montana for California. But I continued to drink. In fact, I drank more than ever. Of course bad things continued to happen, and I eventually reached the point where I just gave in. I'd been in this situation since July 2002, and there was no end in sight. I finally gave up. I accepted the fact that this miserable lifestyle was my destiny. I thought I'd be dead in a year or less, and actually hoped that it would be sooner rather than later.

Before I'd moved to California, though, I reconnected through Facebook with a woman I'd known when we were kids. Even though I was still drinking, we enjoyed long conversations on the phone, just catching up. She even invited me to her home in Georgia for her birthday and Thanksgiving. I wound up going, and we spent two weeks together. Even though she got to see the real me, she still called me once I returned to California. She even asked me to come back for Christmas and New Year's, which I did. All the while I was full-force drinking. I ended up staying with her in Georgia, where I decided to leave my old life behind, lock stock and barrel. Except for the drinking. I held onto that.

We got engaged, and she had to deal with things I am not proud of. Finally, I got some help, after she begged me to. But it wasn't by my choice—she had to rush me to the hospital two different times. The doctors had never seen an alcohol blood level as high as mine was. Well, they had, but only in dead people. They told me during my first stay at the hospital that I shouldn't be alive and most likely wouldn't be if I ever drank again. We left after several days . . . but I started drinking again in the car while she was driving me home.

The second time was several months later, when she had to rush me to the emergency room. After many tests, the doctors thought I had "wet brain," which is irreversible. They were not optimistic. Over the several days that I was in the hospital, I was asked to go into rehab and finally agreed. They weren't taking any chances, so someone drove me there. I planned to leave once I got there, but managed to stick it out.

After a week, I was released and my fiancée came and got me. I'll never forget the ride home. I'd been instructed to go straight to an AA meeting, but I refused. I had all the paperwork and knew where all the meetings were, but I just didn't go. I asked her to drive me right home. I was scared, more scared than ever as I was planning to drink again. I got home but never took that drink. One day turned into two, one week into a month, one month into a year, and one year into several. I have not picked up a drink since that second trip to the hospital and have never attended AA. And it gets easier every day. . . . Why?

Here's why I think I finally mastered failure. After losing everything, I wanted it all back. I knew what I was doing was never going to get me there, but I tried anyway by doing all the wrong things. I forced bad relationships, made bad business decisions and used everything that had happened as an excuse to keep up the anarchy. I refused to let go of my past. I refused to let go of anything. And by not letting go and forcing things, it only got worse. I blamed everyone but myself—my ex, my family, my friends and God. I wanted answers. I wanted to know from God, or anyone, why me? Why Jon? What did I do?

One day, in that last rehab, I lay in bed crying. I remember Johnny Wimbrey saying to me, "Jon, adversity causes some people to break and other people to break records."

Once I finally admitted that there was no going back, that I just had to let go and get on with life, answers started to appear. My relationship with my fiancé improved, my businesses started to flourish, my legal problems went away, and my sanity started to return (although some of my friends might challenge me on that!) Not only did things come back, but problems also started to work themselves out. And these things started to happen so fast I thought I was dreaming.

Life now is better than ever. At the risk of embarrassing myself, I decided to come clean to people about my past. I held nothing back. It's amazing the weight that was lifted by being honest. I was even more amazed how people didn't judge me. They actually accepted me for who I am and seemed okay with the fact that I am not perfect. Some even told me how worried they were for me. People who I once thought would accept me only when I had all the toys, money and all the other junk are actually closer friends now than they were before. Go figure.

I share my story to let you know that you are going to go through many failures even after you think you have arrived. Your failures may be smaller or they may be larger than what I went through. But I'm not going to tell you that if I can get through it, anyone can. I hate that. What I will tell you is this: *You must never let success get to your head.* Learn to be humble if you aren't humble already, and stop trying to recreate good things that happened in your past—those days are gone. Keep the good memories, but don't think of them as something you need to get back to in order for things to move forward. Instead, focus on the new blessings that come into your life. If you keep trying to get back what you once had, you'll miss all the greatness that awaits you in the future.

About Jonathan Gillardi

Jonathan Gillardi was born and raised in the Bronx, New York, and has more than 25 years' experience in high-end financial sales and the network marketing industry. Starting in network marketing at the age of 19, Jon is now a top industry earner and has built organizations of 500,000+ people in more than 70 countries that are responsible for over $100 million in sales.

A sought-after speaker, trainer, consultant and now author, Jon has been a company owner, top distributor and consultant for many large companies. Jon is also a sought-after guest and has appeared on many daytime television talk shows, such as Geraldo and Gordon Elliot, as well as hundreds of weekly radio shows and has been featured in *People* magazine due to his losing over 500 pounds. At one time Jon weighed a massive 652 pounds at only 5'7" tall and had an 88-inch waist. Jon was also the national spokesperson for stomach stapling/gastric bypass in the late 1990s.

"88 Inch Waist" 2.16.93   32" 30 Mths Later

Prior to his now many years of successful marketing experience, Jon was, in his first two years, rookie and sophomore of the year and then youngest sales manager in the history of The Prudential, a 100-year-old, Fortune 100 financial firm—a record that still stands today.

This dynamic speaker has been passionate about helping people since the 1980s when he was in his teens.

Now, by combining his world-class skills and success in social media as well as sales, Internet marketing, coaching and leadership training, he can provide mentoring, national broadcasts, events, tools, training, consulting and leadership to entire companies and network marketing organizations to bring them success.

Jon may be contacted through his website at www.JonGillardi.com, his Twitter page at www.Twitter.com/JGillardi, his Facebook fan page at www.Facebook.com/Gillardi, by Skype @JGillardi, by email at Book@JonGillardi.com or by phone at (949) 468-5884.

Chapter 3

The Only Way Through Is Through
BY JORDAN VARLEY

"Attitude is a little thing that makes a big difference."
- Winston Churchill

When life doesn't work out as you planned, I remember the words of Winston Churchill. Your attitude determines how you react when life throws you a curve. How are you going to catch it? With a positive attitude or a bad one? I was always catching everything with a bad attitude. Had I kept going down the same path, I'm sure that I wouldn't be here to tell my story.

But let me start at the beginning. As a child, I was picked on and bullied, a loner. By the sixth grade, I started to go down a dark road. I hung out with older kids and smoked marijuana and tried other recreational drugs. By 13, I had connections and began dealing marijuana to some of the kids at school. At the time, I felt untouchable because of the money I was making.

At 14, I amassed even more money selling magic mushrooms. I stayed out all the time, partying with the wrong crowd. They seemed to have everything, and I was drawn to that. I had a terrible attitude toward my parents, and nothing could stop me from doing what I wanted.

At 17, I faced an assault charge from a fight I got in. While I got off lucky with probation and community service, I didn't get any smarter. I started doing hard drugs, once even overdosing on cocaine and ecstasy. That was one of the scariest times in my life and a big eye-opener. I stopped doing everything—no more drugs, no more alcohol. I walked away from the whole crowd.

It wasn't easy. I felt stuck with all of the people in the drug-dealing arena, like I'd never be able to escape. I'd made a bad name for myself and faced it everywhere. When I tried to just hang out, I was always pulled back into the direction of drugs and violence. At parties it was still very hard to say no, and like Tony Robbins says, "It's in your moments of decision where your destiny is shaped."

Fortunately, I made another good decision and created a fall-back plan. I decided to be an electrician. A friend's father owned an electrical company and asked me to help him wire a house that would later be donated as a fund-raiser for the local hospital's pediatrics ward. I needed hours toward community service from my earlier trouble, so I figured it would be good for me and also help a great cause.

Finally, I had something that kept me from hanging out with the wrong crowd. The temptation to go back to that life was strong. The money I was earning in a normal job didn't compare to what I'd made selling drugs, but for the first time, I had a sense of self worth and something to be proud of.

I decided to stick with my fall-back plan and completed my first term of trade school in Toronto. Then I moved to London, Ontario, and started intermediate trade school. There I managed to get on the pre-select list to get hired with one of the largest high-voltage companies in Ontario.

I landed the job, but my superintendent thought I had a bad attitude. I didn't realize it at the time, but looking back, I see that it could have been a lot better. It's like the former head of McDonalds, Ray Kroc, said, "You are either green and growing, or ripe and rotten." At that time, I was rotten to the core. I had a lot of growing up to do and slowly started to realize I needed a major attitude adjustment.

By 21, things at the new job were going great … or so I thought. I pushed to do my best and to learn everything I could, but my lust for more money still burned hotly. I hadn't developed the disciplined mindset yet to do what was right, and slowly I started slipping back in with the wrong crowd.

At first it was just going out after work for a beer, but then I started dealing drugs again—marijuana, ecstasy, cocaine and steroids. Yet again, I was headed toward complete destruction. It never occurred to me that my life could be ruined forever. At the same time that I was dealing drugs, I became a third-term apprentice at the new job, and made over $100,000 that year on paper. But I basically never had to touch the money I earned from work because I made so much selling drugs. The bank account just kept climbing, and I spent money foolishly—on whatever I wanted, whenever I wanted it.

Despite my fat bank account, life spiralled downhill. The drugs had a hold on me. I was borderline addicted to cocaine, and at work my attitude was very explosive. I was angry and agitated from the drugs, and I just didn't care about anything.

I started my last term of trade school when I was 24. The advanced classes required a lot of concentration so once again I tried to buckle down and focus, but I wasn't always myself. There were times when no one would hear from me for a week. Sometimes I wished I would just overdose, believing the world would be better without me. But to have pushed my body that far and still be breathing? I knew I must be here for a real reason.

I had many of those defining moments, thinking *Is this all I'll ever be? Just another loser drug addict?* I felt that because I barely passed high school, I could never be more than just average. I was very depressed, but I knew if someone would just help me through this tough time, I'd be alright. One of those moments hit me like a Mac truck when I realized: *The only way through is through.* I had to dig deep down and pull myself through.

I finally made it out of trade school and finished with a 3.8 GPA. I was extremely happy because I never should have lived through the third term, and considering I had almost pulled off a 4.0, I once again felt on top of the world. I felt like a champion and nothing could stop me, but I wondered, *How long would it last?*

At 25, I finally had my certificate of qualification. I was now a licensed construction and maintenance electrician working for a very reputable company. I felt blessed, but I still wasn't making good choices. My actions were leading me to more failure and, amazingly, I didn't see it.

I started dealing more drugs than ever before. Everything that I thought was so great because of the money I was making actually turned me into a very different person. During this time, I was promoted to sub-foreman on the largest high-voltage job in Ontario. But then, in one of the lowest points of my life and because of my bad attitude and some connections I had, I actually put a "hit" on someone with whom I worked.

As if I hadn't been stupid enough just planning the hit, I talked about it to the wrong people. The news made it back to my superintendent, and a week after my promotion I was fired. I tried to fight it, but the case would have gotten very messy so I agreed with the company's lawyers to just let it go. I had called the hit off before it happened, and there was no solid proof against me. Thankfully, charges were never brought against me.

I knew I'd been lucky, but in my mind, my life felt like it was over. I felt like a loser—ruined, broken down and stepped on. I'd lost the job I loved because of my own wrong choices. I had to live with what I chose but came to realize that the law of attraction was true: *What you focus on most expands.* I'd been more focused on the drug game than on doing everything legit, and I'd lost it all. I was a world-class, grade-A loser and deserved what I got.

I now had a mortgage, two cars, and no job. I needed a lot of money and I needed it fast. Believe it or not, I did the unthinkable. I started right back into what I said I wouldn't touch again. I hooked up with some friends who had a drug operation, and every other week for about three months, I flew 50 pounds of marijuana from Vancouver to Toronto. Once again, the money poured in, and I felt like I couldn't be touched.

One day, I switched drug runs with a partner, who needed the money worse than I did. I know that Someone was looking out for me that day, because the guy never came home. He'd been caught at the airport. I was really freaked out that it could have been me. The guy took all the heat, and I never got into trouble. I had agreed to do the run after that one, but needless to say, there were no more runs. We were done and the heat was on. I was actually angry because I didn't know what I was going do for money.

At this time, I was also dealing steroids regularly. I went to see the main leader in the steroid arena out of Hamilton, Ontario, just before leaving for Las Vegas to check out a business venture. Once in Vegas, I was enjoying the conference and learning all about my new business venture when I got a call from someone who had read in the newspaper about a huge steroid and cocaine bust in Hamilton. He said 23 people had been busted. Once again, I was haunted with the thought that it could have been me.

Two times I had dodged a bullet, and I knew there wouldn't be a third. Finally, I smartened up. I said, *That's it, no more drugs, for real this time. No more selling anything unless it's 100% legit.*

To this day, I'm blessed to say that I've stuck by my word. I will never get involved in hustling again.

Sometimes in my chaotic life, I felt like a ping pong ball in the ocean under the mercy of the Lord, being pushed here and there. All along, I just needed to learn that it's the set of my own sail that will take me in the direction I want to go.

I admit it was hard to stay away from the people I'd been hustling with, and I was depressed for a long time. I felt so alone, cutting all my ties. I was trapped between who I was and who I wanted to be, but I knew the only way through was to get out and never look back. Thankfully, I learned to keep my distance from the game I once played.

Life today is a lot different. When I look around, all I see is opportunity.

The inspiration, passion and love from the new friends I've made are incredible. I can't get over how lucky I am to have such wonderful people in my corner, pushing me and helping me grow. There is no obstacle that I can't overcome, they are merely challenges that God has put there to teach me lessons. and then pass those lessons along to others. I know that nothing is impossible—even the word itself says "I'm possible."

To atone for my past, I am helping to build better schools in Guatemala. What a joy and a blessing to help the people in the world who need it most. It's had a huge impact on my life, and on how I look at the world and at money. I realize now that all I truly need is my love for others and to always be happy with what I have. I'm incredibly grateful for my life, and embracing volunteerism has been one of the best choices I have ever made.

Without money, I wouldn't be able to give back in this way. I know that the more money I have, the more I can give. I may not be able to change the whole world, but for some people I can help change their whole world, and that's what means the most to me.

At the start of 2012, I began to focus on the law of attraction, working hard on myself. I focused on developing as an individual and as a leader in a leadership culture. I constantly push myself to be the best at everything I do, and to always be the happiest and nicest person I can be, and to never forget that I once was a hustler in a very dark and gloomy place.

I've been fortunate to have developed an appreciation for leadership qualities. And I'm grateful for leaders who share their wisdom. For example, one of my mentors, Johnny Wimbrey, always tells me, "True character is measured in direct proportion to what you do when no one else is around." In other words, what you do when no one is watching.

No one else can control where you go in life besides you, and what you think will determine where you go. It's like Henry Ford said, "Whether you think you can or whether you think you can't, you're right." The only one who controls your success in life is you.

What I hope you take away from my story is that anyone in a lonely spot can always be turned around with just a little belief in yourself. Stay focused on your goals, push forward through thick and thin toward your dreams, and you will achieve them. Remember: No one can stop you but YOU, so push through it and understand that you will become what you think about most. Stay positive and never quit on yourself. Get out there and go after your dreams and goals.

May God richly bless you.

About Jordan Varley

Jordan Varley is the founder and CEO of Varley's TNT Distributing LTD. As a successful entrepreneur, he coaches a wide number of individuals on overcoming limitations and eliciting fuller potential. In addition, Jordan has empowered countless others through his business and social media outlets, building teams all over the world. His focus is on helping people overcome adversity and raising self-esteem so that each person can become successful.

Chapter 4

An Interview with Jack Canfield

THE INTERVIEW with Jack Canfield by David E. Wright (*Reprinted with the permission of Mr. Canfield*)

David E. Wright (**Wright**)
Today we are talking to Jack Canfield. You probably know him as the founder and co-creator of the New York Times *#1 best-selling* Chicken Soup for the Soul *book series, which currently has 35 titles and 53 million copies in print in over 32 languages. Jack's background includes a BA from Harvard, a Masters from the University of Massachusetts and an Honorary Doctorate from the University of Santa Monica. He has been a high school and university teacher, a workshop facilitator, a psychotherapist, and for the past twenty-five years, a leading authority in the area of self-esteem and personal development. Jack Canfield, welcome to Conversations on Success!*

Jack Canfield (**Canfield**)

Thank you David. It's great to be with you.

Wright

I talked with Mark Victor Hansen a few days ago. He gave you full credit for coming up with the idea of the Chicken Soup *series. Obviously it's made you an internationally known personality. Other than recognition, has the series changed you personally and if so, how?*

Canfield

I would say that it has and I think in a couple of ways. Number one, I read stories all day long of people who've overcome what would feel like insurmountable obstacles. For example we just did a book *Chicken Soup for the Unsinkable Soul*. There's a story in there about a single mother with three daughters. She got a disease and she had to have both of her hands and both of her feet amputated. She got prosthetic devices and was able to learn how to use them so she could cook, drive the car, brush her daughters' hair, get a job, etc. I read that and I think, "God, what would I ever have to complain and whine and moan about?" So I think at one level it's just given me a great sense of gratitude and appreciation for everything I have, made me less irritable about the little things. I think the other thing that's happened for me personally is my sphere of influence has changed. By that I mean I got asked, for example, a couple of years ago to be the keynote speaker to the Women's Congressional Caucus and these are all the women in Congress, Senators, Governors, and Lieutenant Governors in America. I said, "What do you want me to talk about, what topic?" They said, "Whatever you think we need to know to be better legislators." And I thought, "Wow, they want me to tell them about what laws they should be making and what would make a better culture?" Well, that wouldn't have happened if our books hadn't come out and I hadn't become famous. I think I get to play with people at a higher level and have more influence in the world. That's important to me because my life purpose is inspiring and empowering people to live their highest vision so the world works for everybody and I get to do that on a much bigger level than when I was just a high school teacher back in Chicago.

Wright

I think one of the powerful components of that book series is that you can read a positive story in just a few minutes, come back and revisit it. I know my daughter who is 13 now has three of the books and she just reads them interchangeably. Sometimes I go in her bedroom and she'll be crying and reading one of them. Other times she'll be laughing so they really are chicken soup for the soul, aren't they?

Canfield

They really are. In fact we have four books in the *Teenage Soul* series now and a new one coming out at the end of this year. I was talking to one of my sons, I have a son who's 11 and he has a 12-year-old friend who's a girl and we have a new book called *Chicken Soup for the Teenage Soul and the Tough Stuff.* It's all about dealing with parents' divorces, teachers who don't understand you, boyfriends who drink and drive, and stuff like that and I asked her, "Why do you like this book?" because it's our most popular book among teens right now. And she said, "You know whenever I'm feeling down I read it and it makes me cry and I feel better. Some of the stories make me laugh and some of the stories make me feel more responsible for my life. But basically I just feel like I'm not alone." One of the people that I work with recently said that the books are like a support group between the covers of a book, to hear other peoples' experiences and realize you're not the only one going through something.

Wright

Jack, with our Conversations on Success *publication we're trying to encourage people in our audience to be better, to live better and be more fulfilled by listening to the examples of our guests. Is there anything or anyone in your life that has made a difference for you and helped you to become a better person?*

Canfield

Yes and we could do 10 shows just on that. I'm influenced by people all the time. If I were to go way back I'd have to say one of the key influences in my life was Jesse Jackson when he was still a minister in Chicago. I was teaching in an all-black high school there and I went to Jesse Jackson's church with a friend one time. What happened for me was I saw somebody with a vision. This was before Martin Luther King was killed and Jesse was one of the lieutenants in his organization. I just saw people trying to make the world work better for a certain segment of the population. I was inspired by that kind of visionary belief that it's possible to make change. Then later John F. Kennedy was a hero of mine. I was very much inspired by him. Later a therapist by the name of Robert Resnick that I had for two years. He taught me a little formula called E + R = O that stands for Events + Response = Outcome. He said, "If you don't like your outcomes quit blaming the events and start changing your responses." One of his favorite phrases was, "If the grass on the other side of the fence looks greener, start watering your own lawn more." I think it helped me get off of any kind of self-pity I might have had because I had parents who were alcoholics and that whole number. It's very easy to blame them for your life not working. They weren't real successful or rich and I was surrounded by people who were and I felt like, "God, what if I'd had parents like they had? I could have been a lot better." He just got me off that whole notion and made me realize the hand you were dealt is the hand you've got to play and take responsibility for who you are and quit complaining and blaming others and get on with your life. That was a turning point for me. I'd say the last person that really affected me big time was a guy named W. Clement Stone who was a self-made multi-millionaire in Chicago. He taught me that success is not a four-letter word, it's nothing to be ashamed of and you ought to go for it. He said, "The best thing you can do for the poor is not be one of them." Be a model for what it is to live a successful life. So I learned from him the principles of success and that's what I've been teaching now for the last almost 30 years.

Wright

He was the entrepreneur in the insurance industry, wasn't he?

Canfield

He was. He had combined insurance and when I worked for him he was worth 600 million dollars and that was before the dot.com millionaires came along in Silicon Valley. He just knew more about success and he was a good friend of Napoleon Hill who wrote *Think and Grow Rich* and he was a fabulous mentor. I really learned a lot from him.

Wright

I miss some of the men that I listened to when I was a young salesman coming up and he was one of them. Napoleon Hill was another one and Dr. Peale, all of their writings made me who I am today. I'm glad that I got that opportunity.

Canfield

One speaker whose name you probably will remember, Charlie Tremendous Jones, says "Who we are is a result of the books we read and the people we hang out with." I think that's so true and that's why I tell people, "If you want to have high self-esteem hang out with people with high self-esteem. If you want to be more spiritual hang out with spiritual people." We're always telling our children, "Don't hang out with those kids." The reason we don't want them to is we know how influential people are with each other. I think we need to give ourselves the same advice. Who are we hanging out with? We can hang out with them in books, cassette tapes, CDs, radio shows like yours, and in person.

Wright

One of my favorites was a fellow named Bill Gove from Florida. I talked with him about three or four years ago and he's retired now. His mind is still as quick as it ever was. I thought he was one of the greatest speakers I had ever heard. What do you think makes up a great mentor? In other words, are there characteristics that mentors seem to have in common?

Canfield

I think there are two obvious ones. One, I think they have to have the time to do it and two, the willingness to do it. And then three I think they need to be someone who is doing something you want to do. W. Clement Stone used to tell me, "If you want to be rich hang out with rich people. Watch what they do, eat what they eat, dress the way they dress. Try it on." It wasn't like give up your authentic self, but it was that they probably have habits that you don't have. Study them, study the people who are already like you. I always ask salespeople in an organization, "Who are the top two or three in your organization?" I tell them to start taking them out to lunch and dinner and for a drink and finding out what they do. Ask them, "What's your secret?" Nine times out of ten they'll be willing to tell you. It goes back to what we said earlier about asking. I'll go into corporations and I'll say, "Who are the top 10 people?" They'll all tell me and I'll say, "Did you ever ask them what they do different than you?" They go, "No." "Why not?" "Well they might not want to tell me." "How do you know? Did you ever ask them? All they can do is say no. You'll be no worse off than you are now." So I think with mentors you just look at people who seem to be living the life you want to live, achieving the results you want to achieve. And then what we tell them in our book is when you approach a mentor they're probably busy and successful and so they haven't got a lot of time. Just say, "Can I talk to you for 10 minutes every month?" If I know it's only going to be 10 minutes I'll probably say yes. The neat thing is if I like you I'll always give you more than 10 minutes, but that 10 minutes gets me in the door.

Wright

In the future are there any more Jack Canfield books authored singularly?

Canfield

Yes, I'm working on two books right now. One's called E + R = O which is that little formula I told you about earlier. I just feel I want to get that out there because every time I give a speech when I talk about that the whole room gets so that you could hear a pin drop, it gets silent. You can tell that people are really getting value. Then I'm going to do a series of books on the principles of success. I've got about 150 of them that I've identified over the years. I have a book down the road I want to do that's called *No More Put-Downs* which is a book probably aimed mostly at parents, teacher and managers. There's a culture we have now of put-down humor whether it's *Married With Children* or *All in the Family*, there's that characteristic of macho put-down humor. There's research now that's showing how bad it is for kids' self-esteem, co-workers, athletes when the coaches do it so I want to get that message out there as well.

Wright

It's really not that funny, is it?

Canfield

No, we'll laugh it off because we don't want to look like we're a wimp but underneath we're hurt. The research now shows that you're better off breaking a child's bones than you are breaking their spirit. A bone will heal much more quickly than their emotional spirit will.

Wright

I remember recently reading a survey where people listed the top five people that had influenced them in their lives. I've tried it on a couple of groups at church and other places. In my case and also in the survey it's running that about three out of the top five are always teachers. I wonder if that's going to be the same in the next decade.

Canfield

I think probably because as children we're at our most formative years. We actually spend more time with our teachers than we do with our parents. Research shows that the average parent only interacts verbally with each of their children only about eight and a half minutes a day. Yet at school you're interacting with your teacher for anywhere from six to eight hours depending on how long your school day is, and coaches, chorus directors, and all that kind of thing. So I think that in almost everybody's life there's been that one teacher who loved you as a human being and not just a subject matter, some person they were supposed to fill full of History and English. And that person believed in you and inspired you. Les Brown is one of the great motivational speakers in the world. If it hadn't been for one teacher who said, "I think you can do more than be in a special ed. class; I think you're the one," he'd probably still be cutting grass in the median strip of the highways in Florida instead of being a $35,000-a-talk speaker.

Wright

I had a conversation one time with Les when he was talking about this wonderful teacher that discovered that he was dyslexic. Everybody else called him dumb and this one lady just took him under her wing and had him tested. His entire life changed because of her interest in him.

Canfield

I'm on the board of advisors of the Dyslexic Awareness Resource

Center here in Santa Barbara. The reason is I taught high school with a lot of kids who were called at-risk, kids who would end up in gangs and so forth. What we found over and over was that about 78% of all the kids in the juvenile detention centers in Chicago were kids who had learning disabilities, primarily dyslexia, but there were others as well. They were never diagnosed and they weren't doing well in school so they'd drop out. As soon as you drop out of school you become subject to the influence of gangs and other kinds of criminal and drug linked activities. If they had just diagnosed these kids earlier, and there are a lot of really good programs that can teach dyslexics to read and so forth, then we'd get rid of half of the juvenile crime in America.

Wright

My wife is a teacher and she brings home stories that are heartbreaking, about parents not being as concerned about their children as they used to be or at least not as helpful as they used to be. Did you find that to be a problem when you were teaching?

Canfield

It depends on what kind of district you're in. If it's a poor district the parents could be drugged out, on alcohol, not available basically. If you're in a really high-rent district the parents not being available because they're both working, coming home tired, they're jet-setters, they're working late at the office because they're workaholics. Sometimes it just legitimately takes two paychecks to pay the rent anymore. I find that the majority of parents care but often they don't know what to do. They don't know how to discipline their children. They don't know how to help them with their homework. They're not passing on skills that they never got. Unfortunately the trend tends to be like a chain letter. The people with the least amount of skills tend to have the most number of children. The other thing is you get crack babies. In Los Angeles one out of every 10 babies born is a crack baby.

Wright

That's unbelievable.

Canfield

Yes and another statistic is 50% of kids by the time they're 12 years old have started experimenting with alcohol. I see a lot of that in the Bible belt. It's not the big city, urban designer drugs but you get a lot of alcoholism. Another thing you get, unfortunately, is a lot of let's call it familial violence – a lot of kids getting beat up and hit, parents who drink and then explode. And as we talked about earlier child abuse and sexual abuse. You see a lot of that.

Wright

Most people are fascinated by these TV shows about being a survivor. What has been the greatest comeback that you have made from adversity in your career or in your life?

Canfield

You know it's funny, I don't think I've had a lot of major failures and setbacks where I had to start over. My life's been kind of on an intentional curve. But I do have a lot of challenges. Mark and I are always setting goals that challenge us and we always say, "The purpose of setting a really big goal is not so that you can achieve it so much, but it's who you become in the process of achieving it." A friend of mine Jim Rose says, "You want to set goals big enough so that in the process of achieving them you become someone worth being." I think that to be a millionaire is nice but so what? People make the money, they lose it. People get the big houses, they burn down or Silicon Valley goes belly up and all of a sudden they don't have a big house anymore. But who you became in the process of learning how to do that can never be taken away from you. So what we do is we constantly put big challenges in front of us. Right now we have a book coming out in a month called *Chicken Soup for the Teacher's Soul.* You'll have to make sure to get a copy for your wife. I was a teacher and I was a teacher trainer for years. But in the last seven years, because of the success of the *Chicken Soup* books I haven't been in the education world that much. So I've got to go out and relearn how do I market to that world? I met with a Superintendent of Schools. I met with a guy named Jason Dorsey who's one of the number one consultants in the world in that area. I found out who has the best-selling book in that area. I sat down with his wife for a day and talked about her marketing approaches. So I believe that if you face any kind of adversity, whether it's you lose your job, your husband dies, you get divorced, you're in an accident like Christopher Reeves and become paralyzed, or whatever, you simply do what you have to do. You find out who's already handled this and how did they do it. Then you find out either from their book or from their tape or by talking to them or interviewing them, and you get the support you need to get through it. Whether it's a counselor in your church or you go on a retreat or you read the Bible. You do something that gives you the support you need to get to the other end and you have to know what the end is that you want to have. Do you want to be remarried? Do you just want to have a job and be a single mom? What is it? If you reach out and ask for support I think people really like to help other people. They're not always available because sometimes they're going through it. But there's always someone with a helping hand. Often I think we let our pride get in the way. We let our stubbornness get in the way. We let our belief in how the world should be get in our way instead of dealing with how the world is. When we get that out of the way then we can start doing that which we need to do to get where we need to go.

Wright

If you could have a platform and tell our audience something that you feel that would help or encourage them, what would you say?

Canfield

I'd say number one, believe in yourself and believe in your dreams, and trust your feelings. I think too many people are trained like when they're little kids and they're mad at their daddy, they're told, "You're not mad at your Daddy." They go, "Gee, I thought I was." Or you say, "That's going to hurt." The doctor says, "No it's not." Then they give you the shot and it hurts. They say, "See that didn't hurt, did it?" You start not to trust yourself. Or you say to your mom, "Are you upset?" and the mom says, "No" when she really is. So you stop learning to trust your perception. I tell the story over and over there are hundreds of people I've met who've come from upper-class families where they make big incomes and the dad's a doctor, and the kid wants to be a mechanic and work in an auto shop because that's what he loves. The family says, "That's beneath us. You can't do that." So the kid ends up being an anesthesiologist killing three people because he's not paying attention. What he really wants to do is tinker with cars. I tell people you've got to trust your own feelings, your own motivations, what turns you on, what you want to do, what makes you feel good, and quit worrying about what other people say, think, want for you. Decide what you want for yourself and then do what you need to do to go about getting it. It takes work. I always tell people that I read a book a week minimum and at the end of the year I've read 52 books. We're talking about professional books, books on self-help, finances, psychology, parenting, and so forth. At the end of 10 years you've read 520 books. That puts you in the top 1% of people knowing stuff in this country. But most people are spending their time watching TV. W. Clement Stone told me when I went to work for him, "I want you to cut out one hour a day of TV." I said, "OK, what do I do with it?" He said, "Read." He told me what kind of stuff to read. He said, "At the end of a year you'll have spent 365 hours reading. Divide that by a 40-hour work week and that's nine-and-a-half weeks of education every year." I thought, "Wow, that's two months." It's like going back to summer school. As a result of that I have close to 8,000 books in my library. The reason I'm on your show instead of someone else is that people like me and Jim Rohn and Les Brown and you, read a lot. We listen to tapes and we go to those seminars. That's why we're the people with the information. I always say that your raise becomes effective when you do. You'll become more effective as you gain more skills, more insight, and more knowledge.

Wright

Jack, I have watched your career for over a decade and your accomplishments are just outstanding. But your humanitarian efforts are really what impress me. I think that you're doing great things, not only in California, but all over the country.

Canfield

It's true. In addition to all of the work we do we have all of our books. We pick one to three charities and we've given away over six million dollars in the last eight years, along with our publisher who matches every penny we give away. We've planted over a million trees in Yosemite National Park. We've bought hundreds of thousands of cataract operations in third-world countries. We've contributed to the Red Cross, the Humane Society, and on it goes. It feels like a real blessing to be able to make that kind of a contribution in the world.

Wright

Today we have been talking to Jack Canfield, the founder and cocreator of the Chicken Soup for the Soul *book series, which currently has 35 titles and I'll have to update this. It was 53 million. How many has it been now, Jack?*

Canfield

We're almost up to 78 million. We have a book coming out in just a couple of weeks called *Chicken Soup for the Soul of America*. It's all stories that grew out of September 11th and it's a real healing book for our nation. I would encourage your listeners to get themselves a copy and share it with their families.

Wright

I will stand in line to get one of those. Thank you so much being with us on Conversations on Success.

About Jack Canfield

Jack Canfield is one of America's leading experts on developing self esteem and peak performance. A dynamic and entertaining speaker, as well as a highly sought-after trainer, he has a wonderful ability to inform and inspire audiences toward developing their own human potential and personal effectiveness.

Jack Canfield is most well-known for the *Chicken Soup for the Soul* series, which he co-authored with Mark Victor Hansen, and for his audio programs about building high self-esteem. Jack is the founder of Self-Esteem Seminars, located in Santa Barbara, California, which trains entrepreneurs, educators, corporate leaders and employees how to accelerate the achievement of their personal and professional goals. Jack is also the founder of The Foundation for Self Esteem, located in Culver City, California, which provides self-esteem resources and training to social workers, welfare recipients and human resource professionals.

Jack graduated from Harvard in 1966, received his M.E. degree at the University of Massachusetts in 1973, and an Honorary Doctorate from the University of Santa Monica. He has been a high school and university teacher, a workshop facilitator, a psychotherapist, and for the past 30 years, a leading authority in the area of self-esteem and personal development.

As a result of his work with prisoners, welfare recipients and inner-city youth, Jack was appointed by the state legislature to the California Task Force to Promote Self-Esteem and Personal and Social Responsibility. He also served on the board of trustees of the National Council for Self-Esteem.

Jack Canfield
P.O. Box 30880
Santa Barbara, CA 93130
Email: info4jack@jackcanfield.com

Chapter 5

Spectators
BY MATT MATTHEWS

"Nothing can add more power to your life than concentrating all your energies on a limited set of targets."

- Nido Qubein

Imagine it with me: There I was, at one end of a soccer pitch standing by the goal with the ball at my feet. My coach had promised a reward if I could score a goal in the opposite end within two minutes. There was nobody else on the pitch but me; all I had to do was dribble the ball to the other end and kick it in. Easy, right? Now, although I was alone on the field itself, a fair number of people stood at both sidelines throughout the entire length of it, just watching.

Nervously, I began to dribble down the pitch. That's when one of the spectators rudely shouted out, "It's not possible; you should quit!" An other one said, "What's the point? It's not worth it!" And before long, a lot of them had joined in. I heard things like, "You won't get any reward even if you do score the goal!"; "I tried and failed, so will you!"; "Don't be silly, be realistic!" and many other discouraging remarks.

As I got about a quarter of the way down the pitch, I looked up and saw a close friend in the crowd. He had one of those "what's the point?" expressions on his face. Uncertain myself of how great the reward was going to be, I momentarily lost focus. I paused and went over to him to see if he knew what the reward was, and if there was really any point to this task at all. That's when I felt something hit my back. I turned around, initially confused, and saw an eggshell on the ground. Looking over to the opposite sideline, I saw someone pointing at me, laughing. The smug punk was just standing there, rudely laughing and pointing! *How dare he?* I thought, the focus of scoring my goal now slipping ever further to the background of my attention.

I began making my way back across the field to tell him off, when yet another object hit my back! This one really hurt! I paused, turned around, and saw a whole apple rolling away. It had been hurled by someone at the first sideline. Of course, I now began to head in that direction again. But with all my back and forth from sideline to sideline, I was spending so much time with the spectators that, before I could accomplish anything, my two minutes were up—and I was goalless. I never did find out what my reward would have been, and all because of my own lack of focus and determination.

Of course, the details of this story aren't really true. That is, these things didn't happen exactly as I've described, but on a certain level they are happening to many of us, every day. Think of the soccer pitch as our own playing field; the apples and eggs as doubts and criticisms; the goal as our vision; and of course, the spectators are *still* the spectators.

In retrospect, throughout my younger years, I wasted a lot of time and energy engaging in unnecessary debates with those who had many doubts and criticisms, but who in reality were no more qualified than I was in the given area.

I recall one of my teachers saying to me when I was fourteen years old, that if I didn't stop talking in class and get on with my work, I would never get a decent job when I was older. I retorted that I would start my own company and therefore wouldn't need a job. I then crossed a line, "Sir, I might even hire you one day to train my staff." Unsurprisingly, that quip got me an hour's detention after school. That day, there were three other pupils in detention along with me. Afterward, we got to talking about what we were going to be when we left school. Again, I asserted that I was going to start my own company. One of the other students, Phillip, turned to me and said, "My dad set up his own company, and he's struggling. It's really hard. My dad said that 95% of new companies fail in their first year." Phillip conveyed this information with absolute conviction.

Walking home, I replayed his words over and over in my mind, consciously unaware that in doing so I was only reinforcing them and slowly beginning to accept them as true. Those words became a part of my belief system for the next seven years, until I finally pushed past my fear of failure based on that conversation with Phillip, and set up my first company, which I kept for three years, proving him wrong.

When I actually left secondary school, I did so prematurely due to being permanently excluded for constantly disregarding the "authority" of the teachers. If truth be told I considered myself somewhat a freethinker, and as such I partially despised the confines of an enforced regime. Since I was permanently excluded early, no exams were taken, and therefore no exams were passed. I considered enrolling in my local college to catch up on my grades; however, I was also eager to experience the world at large and earn a living for myself, so despite having told my teacher that I wouldn't need a job, I went and looked for exactly that—a job.

It wasn't long before that teacher's words came back to haunt me. I began to realize just how tough it was to get a decent job without any grades. I landed a couple of retail jobs, but found it rather challenging to conform to the typical 9-to-5 routine. I also despised being abrasively bossed about by my seniors. Needless to say, those retail positions didn't last long. I tried a few door-to-door sales and telemarketing positions, all of which failed for the same reasons. Of course I wanted to earn money, but I also desired the freedom to come and go as I pleased. I chose freedom, and once again I was unemployed.

Finding it increasingly difficult to wriggle my way into a job, after a fair share of setbacks I began to lose hope. I sought social refuge among some other young people who also felt defeated, and after being introduced to friends of friends, one thing led to another. Soon, I was hanging with the wrong crowd. During this period, I had also decided to move away from home despite being advised by various family members not to. So at seventeen, I packed my bags and went to stay with a friend. The downward spiral only continued, and before long I had lost friends to gang violence and found myself in and out of police custody. I had also been subjected to a couple of near-death experiences, and subsequently had turned to using drugs as a form of escape from the mental stress and emotional pain. Days turned to weeks, weeks into months, and months into a couple of years. At this point, under the surface, I was masking a deep-rooted feeling of disappointment in myself because I had lost my will to *participate* in building my dream. Instead, I was merely *spectating*. I felt that I had truly "mastered failure."

Something had to change, and that something was my mindset. I was at the point where enough was enough. I felt that I had more to give, but didn't know where to start. The next morning I woke up and made a firm decision that would change the course of my life forever. I took a personal vow to first stop smoking and to keenly focus on improving my diet. Then I made a firm commitment: Never again would I do, be or give less than I could. Looking in the mirror, I told myself, *"The only one stopping you, is you."*

As soon as I made that commitment, I began relentlessly acting upon it and things started to fall into place. Exactly one week later, I successfully landed a sales position within a telecommunications company. Every fibre of my body focused on positively implementing effective strategies for an empowering change. After just a week with that company, I stumbled upon a simple strategy which I implemented to astonishing effect. My sales went through the roof. Everybody wanted to know how I was breaking all the records, so when I was finished feeling like "the man," I showed them.

It was simple. I had stopped using the company's supplied data of numbers to call, but instead worked solely on recommendations. Every prospect that I approached, without exception, was on the basis of them having been referred by a friend of theirs who had already made a purchase. I would get from each client the contact details of at least 10 to 20 of their friends, sometimes even their whole phonebook. I was creating my own database. No more cold calling; I was now warm calling, armed with the name and recommendation of the prospect's friend. As far as I was concerned, the company's cold-calling data were now obsolete—and of course they didn't argue with that. This simple amendment in the approach took the company's gross volume of telephone connections from an average of 110 per week to 470 per week, but I wasn't prepared for what would happen next.

One night on my way home, I was randomly stopped and searched by two police officers. With nothing to hide, I gave my name and the officer ran it through the system. It turned out that I still had a warrant, which I was completely unaware of, for a minor offense two years earlier when I'd been stopped with a small bag of marijuana. At the time, it was so minor that I was convinced it would be dropped, so I had forgotten all about it.

Nonetheless, when the officer confirmed the warrant, I was taken to the station and spent the night there. The next morning in the magistrate's court was like the worst scene in a movie. The judge remanded me back into custody! I looked at her with complete disbelief. After having got myself back on track, now this? So I was held for fourteen days until the case was dismissed. Once I was discharged, I contacted my employer immediately but was told that I had been replaced. It appeared that they now had the system which quadrupled their connectivity rate, and therefore I was easily disposable. I was devastated.

Recalling the vow I had taken that morning before the mirror, I headed home to scour the local newspaper for another opportunity. I soon found an ad for a small company in need of a sales staff, so I contacted them and was selected for an interview. Later that day, I mentioned to a couple of associates what had happened and told them about my upcoming interview for the sales position. One of them replied, "Sales? Aren't sales jobs for losers?" I know, I know, spectators right? I didn't let his attitude affect mine.

I started my new job the following Monday, and as if by a stroke of luck, on that very day I sold a product that the director himself had labelled a tough sell. It wasn't that I was particularly good at selling at that point, but more that the customer just happened to be in the mood to buy and probably would have bought anything. Nonetheless, that sale boosted my early credibility within the company, and before long I was the top salesperson.

Within six months, I was promoted to manager and given the task of recruiting and training a sales force. My perseverance had paid off; it was time to shine. I took all of the frustration and energy from those wasted years and channelled it into one focus—success. I intensely studied some the top communicators and over time developed an enhanced communication skills training program, which was another massive success within that company and others. By six months from that point, I had managed to take this small company's net profit from £8000.00 per month to £78,000.00 per month—almost a 1000% increase on profit.

Two years later I parted from that company to finally start a business of my own. I then branched out into coordinating various community initiatives, group mentoring and personal coaching as well as writing. These are opportunities that would have never materialized had I continued the needless debating with spectators, or not faced my own fear of failure. Throughout life, if we constantly shy away from new endeavours because of fear, then we also sacrifice innumerable opportunities to learn and grow that often arise *disguised* as failure.

We all have inner genius, moments where we experience truly extraordinary ideas—ideas that, if acted upon with resoluteness, can dramatically increase the quality of our lives. But sometimes we internalize the negative opinions of others, subsequently causing those ideas to fade away. If you have a dream, never let anyone tell you that *you can't*. As the old English proverb states, *"Where there is a will, there is a way."*

I'll close with another imaginary scenario. Pretend that you're travelling on a railway train, sitting in a seat facing the opposite direction from which the train is headed. Though the train is moving forward, all you can see is the past view. How many of us are on that train in life, heading forward but looking backwards, wasting valuable time on needless debate with spectators? Every single day, we're creating our tomorrow. We've all faced inopportune circumstances in the past, but those circumstances do not have to determine our future. Always remember that it's the decisions we are making *right now* that will determine where we'll go. You, too, may one day say *"I have mastered failure, but look at me now."*

About Matt Matthews

Matt Matthews is a London-based self-help author, inspirational speaker and peak performance strategist. Based around the topics covered within his book, *The Only One Stopping You Is You!,* Matt coaches a wide number of individuals on a personal basis toward overcoming limitations and utilising fuller potential. In addition to this, Matt is also the founder and CEO of *Matt Matthews Enterprises,* which is a personal development organisation with one branch specialising in personal coaching and peak performance strategies for young men aged 21 to 35; and the other branch specialising in corporate training programmes such as; Advanced Sales Techniques, Advanced Communications and Thought Leading Services. With over 12 years of experience within the personal development field, Matt has also empowered many people through his instrumental roles in a number of community-based initiatives for overcoming adversity and raising self-esteem.

MATT MATTHEWS ENTERPRISES
UNIT/OFFICE 36,   T: +4420 3292 1391
88 - 90 HATTON GARDEN   M: +4479 2803 4994
FARRINGDON   F: +4420 3292 1391
CENTRAL LONDON   E: admin@mattmatthews.co
EC1N 8PN   W: www.mattmatthews.co

Chapter 6

Survival of the Fittest

Adapted from *Dessert Travels Well*

BY MATTIE MEACHAM

My goodness, how time flies; another year is almost over. I can't believe it. I'm 46 years old, and I need to get a job! Well, with a ninth-grade education, I know there are not a lot of people who would hire me. But there's one thing I know that I can do, and that's sell. I really hate having to work outside the home and leaving my youngest daughter. I just don't have any other options. She is certainly one of my special gifts and one of my special challenges. A special gift because she is truly a blessing—I would hate to think of my life without her. A special challenge because, at the time that I was pregnant with her, my oldest was getting married, (yes I went to his wedding pregnant) and my youngest was 17. She is only nine now, and I and I hate leaving her and her dad every day.

Also, I'll have to hire someone to clean the house, but that's just a small item to work out.

There is also the issue of my husband's kidney treatments. We've been trained to do them at home. I was surprised that I could learn to stick him and hook him up to the machine. Well I can! (Even though I am a bit challenged when it comes to machines.)

An important part of our kidney-patient training is to go to a psychologist. The good Dr. Kleinpeter—"Clean Peter"! Oh, how we laughed about that poor man's name!—was very impressed with my understanding of the English language. He said I had a "college-level comprehension." He wanted to know how I accomplished that since I certainly did not go to college or even finish high school. I explained to him that I read every day, primarily from the Bible and *The Watchtower* and *Awake!* magazines.

That reminds me: We still are not through with our training. So I will have to work that in along with traveling all over the Texas panhandle to sell insurance.

So here I am, thinking about going back to work just long enough to pay off some debts. My husband couldn't hold up to working much; he has polycystic kidneys and takes dialysis treatment three days a week. A transplant is not an option for him; he doesn't want someone else's body parts. Instead, he felt the machine would be best for him. Every other weekday it's an hour to rinse and get ready for his treatments, four hours hooked up to the machine to clean his blood, and another hour to clean and put the machine away. Well that's the routine, and we do the treatments at home because he can have more control that way.

OK, the next step is to call my son Dallas; he works at this insurance company and does really well. His boss, Wayne tried to talk me into going to work there before, but my son always talked me out of it because I didn't want to work full-time. "Besides," I would think, "what do I know about selling insurance?" (Now here comes that stinkin' thinkin' cropping up again.) "What? And how can I even do that job? It requires a lot of traveling!" (I can be pretty good at stinkin' thinkin' sometimes.) "Besides, my husband was the man in our family, with his gift of gab. What was I? Just some 15-year-old girl who didn't have many social skills. I was only good for hiding Mama's secrets." (I came from a family who had secrets.) "I was only good to keep peace in the family, not the type to sell. Why, I didn't even like people, much less want to try to sell anything to them." (I did *not* want to be all "social.")

"Wait a minute, quit thinking that way." (I had to get my mindset right again.) "You know you aren't shy, only introverted. And you were, after all, the top sales person selling those high-dollar water filters."

Sometimes you just have to remind yourself. "Remember? You also sold faucet units at $10,000 a pop when people came in answering that blind ad. And my goodness, you owned and single-handedly ran a waterbed and furniture store on your own."

Face the thing you fear the most, and the death of fear is certain! "Remember how you felt when Wayne, the sales manager ran out of the restaurant to catch you so he could offer you a job selling insurance? That shows you can do it; just believe!" After all, I had been in sales, even owned my own waterbed and furniture store, which I successfully ran as a totally debt-free business. I'd also been very successful at a business where we placed ads in the newspaper, inviting people to a seminar to sell them on the idea of investing $10,000 in a water filter business. So I knew I could do this too. (Just believe.)

Just believe!

"OK, here goes. I'm going to call my son," and I did. "Well, son, your dad and I have gotten into debt, and I need to work for about six months. No, I don't want to go to the company convention, just to the training class and then get to work. No, I have not talked to your boss, just to you. I can go the first week in January. Yes, I know it's Christmas; that means he's at home! Just call him!" And call he did.

So started my career with a male-dominated company, calling on businesses to sell them cancer and heart policies, collecting the first month's payment and setting up their bank drafts.

So what pearls of wisdom do I have to offer? Remember: *Even if you are afraid and don't feel worthy, you will never achieve or gain anything if you don't just do it.* (I know you expected me to say TRY to do it, but I don't believe in TRYING; only DOING.) How many times have you heard someone say, and it's always with a bit of a whine in their voice, they'll say, "But I'm TRYING!" To which I say, "Just do it!"

Now, will you always be successful in another person's eyes? Of course not, but success is measured differently by all. Some people measure success by how much money they make, but I measure success by the happiness I see in a person's eyes and in their whole demeanor.

It's tough, I know. Success can be elusive. But only through enduring your personal climb up "the mountain," with a heavy backpack AND walking tall as you journey through your own personal "Death Valley" with sweat on your back, will you truly savor and enjoy your stroll along the cool, soft and beautiful "beach of success." Remember, it's the journey that makes the woman or the man!

Another important thing keep in mind is this: When you are starting a new project, job or just working through adversities, even if you have had former experience, even if you were expert at your previous opportunity, always attack it like you were totally brand-new. Learn all you can from this new guru if you are fortunate enough to have one, because most definitely you will need their wisdom and handy tricks later. Remember, we are in constant training, even if we are smart! So you especially want and need what they have to offer. You want to have this reservoir of someone else's experience. Do not waste your time or theirs; respect what they have to offer.

But back to my story. Just getting to my training class presented a hardship. We were so broke, and we'd just burned up the motor in our second car. I had to drive our only car to Dallas, six hours away, and leave my family afoot for a week. I had just enough money to eat breakfast only. At the hotel, they had happy-hour hors d'oeuvres in the bar, and that was the other meal I ate each day. But I made it through, and everyone survived.

So, as I said before, I started from the bottom doing exactly as I was taught in the training, and made my first commission check of $1,200 that first week in the field. I drove to work every morning and met the team at 8:30. In order to be on time, I had to get up about 5:00 to drive an hour and half. Then, in the evenings on Mondays, Wednesdays and Fridays, I made sure to get home by 6:30 to start the five-hour process of my husband's dialysis treatments on the kidney machine.

I tell you all this to illustrate the kinds of the things you may have to do—and to warn you that things can get in your way if you let them. In order to reach your goals, you may simply have to find ways around or put in more hours than the other guy or girl. *Do not allow the everyday things in life to get in the way of accomplishing your goals.*

So my first week was pretty awesome, but what about the weeks after that?

That first year I made over $75,000 and bought my husband and my-self new cars. I had written down my goals for that year, and when I checked, I'd met them all in just six months—that was six months ahead of schedule!

So began my 22-year career in the insurance business, that started as a short-term thing to pay off some bills, as I said before a very male-dominated business. I became a sales manager within three years. I was offered the position before then, but mainly because of my husband's health and having a young daughter at home, I waited.

I was promoted to regional manager, and then climbed to state manager, becoming the first woman in the company to do so. I moved to Louisiana and managed all of Louisiana and East Texas. I was the company's number-one manager that year and developed regional managers who led a minimum of three to four teams each.

As time went on (a little over a year), I managed to develop my area, with the help of my recruiter, to five teams with 5–10 agents on each team. I might mention that mine was a multimillion-dollar area then. Also, all of my regional managers were men, and I believe I earned their respect because of my work ethic.

However, that was not the end of my struggles. Many times struggles come from within. You know, the old self-doubt—the past coming back to surround you, the regrets over what you have done and what you haven't. How do you quiet that accusing inner voice? In the same way you quiet the voices that try to hold you back on the outside. It's through what I call self-talk. The reality is *I deserve to be loved and to be whole in my mind, body and spirit.* Affirmations can be especially help-ful just before you go to sleep. Quietly repeat them to yourself every evening. A whole book could be written on the benefits of affirmations.

Now back to my story. I had two divisions that I was running very successfully, but then a change shook up our company. It was sold to a large corporation, and my new boss replaced me with a young man who had been in our business only three months. It was a real slap in the face for me. Everything I'd built was gone. It was one of the toughest times in my whole career.

So after licking my wounds for a while, I picked up and moved to Dallas-Ft. Worth to tackle a new challenge and start from the ground up, again. The entire area only had one other person besides me. Within about six months, we went from one agent to 20 reps. I was put in charge of most of Texas and all of New Mexico.

Well, about the time I was to be promoted, my boss was fired, and I was instead offered a "great new opportunity." I say that to make lemonade out of lemons. My "new opportunity" was really a complete transformation. I had to take a step back, but I started building another new team, and within a year had taken a nonproducing area and had it back in the multimillions.

Where there is adversity, there is an opportunity for growth. It may sound like a contradiction, but adversity is a tool that can be used to either make us or break us. I have had a lot of tests and adversity in my life, including the time I saw my mom hit my dad on the head, again and again, until he passed out. That was the first one I can remember, but one of my greatest tests was when I lost my son. During that awful period, it was an enormous struggle to just live. I really thought I would die. That's something that will always be there, but somehow you learn to live with it.

I have the same struggles that most of us have. It is not the action that can get us; it's our reaction to it. I chose to react in a positive way to negative situations a long time ago. I think somehow it was born in me. I'm the type to greet you with a smile and say, "I'm so glad to see you!"

That's pretty much my story. A 90-pound, 15-year-old girl decided to dance naked in a field after her boyfriend gave her a beer. She danced around and around and around. No surprise, she got pregnant, and thus began the life of a young girl and an 18-year-old boy and their future together.

She became the woman with a ninth-grade education who built a multimillion-dollar business with the same company, twice.

About Mattie Meacham

Mattie Meacham grew up in Amarillo, Texas. She was married on her sixteenth birthday and had three children by the age of 19. Twenty years later, she had her fourth child. She and her husband, Ted, were married for more than 30 years until he died of polycystic kidney disease.

She has owned and operated her own retail stores and has trained hundreds of successful salespeople. She has built, trained and developed successful sales organizations all over the U.S. She is called on to speak, train and motivate sales professionals nationwide.

She is currently married to John Meacham and resides in the Dallas–Ft. Worth area. She has four children, nine grandchildren and two beagles, George and Gracie.

Chapter 7

Personal Development 101
BY CJ PETERSON

"I was an overnight success all right, but 30 years is a long, long night."

- Ray Kroc

Just last year, I was questioning the path I was on. I was doubting the choices I'd made and beating myself up for every decision that brought me to this point. For the first time, I truly had a sense of what depression looked and felt like. Most people would say I'm an optimistic and positive person, but I felt like a complete failure.

My high school and college friends were cranking in business, in great relationships, starting families, while I was living at my parents' house rent-free and single because I couldn't afford anything else. My credit cards were maxed out, and I couldn't even afford to fill up my gas tank. I had just under $40,000 of total debt—$30,000 on my credit cards alone. For more than 18 months, I struggled, juggled and maneuvered to keep myself afloat. Few people knew about the pit I was in, because I kept my attitude up. Everyone loves a success story, but the time to share is *after* you've won the victory.

When I pictured myself at 31, I would see someone in the prime of life, not feeling tired, exhausted and burnt out—yet that's how I felt. It got so bad that I did something I said I would never do. Every weekend for two summers, I made the five-hour drive up to northern Minnesota to help manage my parent's Dairy Queen to make a few extra bucks. That may not sound bad, but I'd grown up for 20 years in Dairy Queens, telling my parents I'd NEVER take them over. It was a big blow to my pride when I had to go back in order to cover my bills. Every weekend I got to eat humble pie, but thankfully my parents didn't rub it in.

Even though I was living with them, I never told my parents how bad it was. I didn't want them to worry or feel like they needed to help me out more. They have always been supportive of my entrepreneurial spirit (thank God), but I was shocked that they didn't push me harder to go into corporate sales sooner when my business dreams weren't working out.

Thankfully, given the title of this book, you know my story turns around. The question is, how did things shift so quickly? How did I make more in two months than I did in more than two years *and* wipe out all my debt? The even more interesting question is, how, after struggling so much in business, was I able to achieve such a high level of success?

What preceded my "overnight success" is a LONG journey that deepened my faith in God, developed my character, refined my skills, set the foundation for success and tested my commitment to living a fulfilled life. I love the quote by Ray Kroc, founder of McDonalds, about overnight success. "I was an overnight success all right, but 30 years is a long, long night." I now understand a little about how Mr. Kroc must have felt and know the truth behind "overnight success is never overnight." Let me add some color to this picture.

During college I worked weekends as a server, went to every leadership program I could, and helped the entrepreneurial club become the largest club on campus at the University of Minnesota. In my junior year though, I went from being the "poster child for the undergraduate student body" (according to an alumni rep at the Dean's office), on a full academic and leadership scholarship, to feeling like an outcast. That year, a peer wrote to our Associate Dean of Undergrad studies recommending I be kicked out or "fixed" because I was involved in "pyramid businesses" (network marketing) and "cult programs" (Landmark Education, a personal training and development company). I was angry, heartbroken, scared of losing my scholarship and felt like my identity was being directly attacked by someone I considered a close friend.

Fortunately, I've had some great mentors like "Famous" Dave Anderson of Famous Dave's of America Bar-B-Que. Late that night I called him, angry and unsure of what to do. He invited me to his house, and when I got there he laughed at the whole situation. He told me "Good job!" about shaking things up and that if I wasn't making a scene then I wouldn't *be* seen. . . . Basically, welcome to the life of an entrepreneur!

What motivated me even more was when the Associate Dean of Marketing said that network marketing isn't a valid business. You see, not only had I grown up in a traditional business family, but my parents always had a network marketing business on the side. I remember going to meetings with my dad and grandpa as a teenager. They would tell me that I could be that guy on stage, that I could have that success story. So now, not only did I have a friend from school bashing me, but the school itself was essentially saying that what I was doing was a scam.

Once again, I sought emotional support and encouragement from my mentors, this time Mary and Warren Nelson. Before network marketing, Mary had been a top real estate agent and Warren a CEO with a Harvard MBA. They've been full-time in the home-based business arena for over 20 years and have made several million dollars. Thank God that Warren and Mary, not my school, shaped my perception of network marketing. They had won the rat race, and then gave it up for network marketing. I saw how they lived and the impact they made in the world. Even though I shed tears and was upset with my school, this experience ultimately only strengthened me.

Today, I want to personally thank my friend and my school for giving me that extra motivation to become even more successful in my chosen career and strengthening my resolve at 20 years old to follow my dreams.

Even though I kept my full-ride scholarship, graduated with honors and had numerous opportunities to enter into the corporate world, I said "no." Instead, I took a huge pay cut, lived at my parents' place and worked a $9-an-hour retail job so I could build my business.

The sacrifice paid off. In 2004, I caught lightning in a bottle. Between 2004 and 2008, our company went from roughly $2 million a month to over $25 million a month.

Following Warren's leadership, at 25 years old, I was full-time in our business and moved out of my parents' place. I was the young gun in our company as the top producer under 30 and won award trips around the world. Life was good; I had it by the tail.

Over the next couple of years, I made more than I would have in most corporate positions, but never got to the $20,000- to $100,000-a-month incomes I envisioned and saw others achieving. Also, I made the big mistake of not saving my money, thinking the business would go on forever. When the economy collapsed in 2008, along with missteps by the company, I watched everything I'd built essentially evaporate over the next two years. By the end of 2009, I'd sold everything I had accumulated and was back at mom and dad's to cut expenses while I attempted to hold onto and resuscitate my business. By May 2010, my heart and hope with that company were ripped to shreds. My business disintegrated and I was done. I now had a choice. Was I going to be bitter and complain the rest of my life about what could have been? Or would I pick myself up, take the good from the situation and keep moving? I chose the latter.

Fortunately, I had another personal friend and mentor, Brian Brooks, who continually reminded me to focus inwardly on my growth and not be controlled by the outward experiences of life. Thank God I had his support, along with people like my parents, Warren and Mary, and a few other tight friends, because over the next two years I was stripped of my pride, hit rock bottom and was brought to my knees.

During those two years, I just couldn't get ahead. From May 2010 to October 2011, I tried two other network marketing companies, worked for my parents at their DQ and helped launch a digital marketing firm with a couple partners. I fought constantly to keep my emotions in check. I lost my confidence at different times and questioned what my purpose was. Sometimes I just wanted to fall asleep and dream my pain away, but I knew that wasn't an option. Many times, my life felt like I was walking through drying cement, but I just kept slogging. I had to keep pushing and stay active—something would open up.

During these times, I had more heartfelt conversations with God than ever before. I truly believed that he wouldn't deal me anything that I couldn't handle and that these experiences would somehow connect together and make me stronger. I have seen throughout my life that everything works together for good; God always provides. I knew deep down that these times of trial would be no different. I kept reminding myself of two quotes I heard from Pastor Randy Morrison at Speak the Word. "You don't know what kind of tea bag you are until you're in some hot water," and "The money can only come after the test in 'test-i-mony.'"

But with more bills than income in October 2011, and no sign of anything turning around, my patience and faith grew tired. I had hit rock bottom and was at my breaking point. I'd flirted with getting a corporate job for a couple of months, and now it was time. I no longer resisted getting a job—and it was at that point my life turned on a dime.

Just a few days after coming to grips with the status of my life, I got a call from Jon Gillardi. Even though we owned an LLC together through another business, Jon and I had never met in person.

Jon told me that he would be flying to Philadelphia to potentially do some consulting for an energy company. The co-founder of this company was on the corporate staff of the wellness company I'd caught lightning in a bottle when I was 25. I had been ignoring his texts, calls and emails for months and now all of a sudden I was on a conference call with him and Jon. They both wanted me to fly out to Philadelphia. At that point, I wasn't really interested because my mindset wasn't right. However, two days later I got a call from another friend who had also been on the corporate staff of that wellness company. He told me how he'd left his VP of Sales job to be a master associate for the same energy company. Now, in three days, I'd heard from three different people I respected, about the same company. None of them truly knew where I was in life. I agreed to fly to Philadelphia.

Long story short, the company looked good. We went from thinking about consulting to deciding to actually build an organization. We started our independence on November 2. I had life. I had hope. I had an opportunity I could sink my teeth into. And for the next eight weeks, we worked 18+ hours a day building our business. The TV that I'd been watching was no longer important. Thoughts of negativity went out the window. I jumped in with both feet, and did phone calls back to back to back with Jon as we built out the business. If you've read Jon's story, you know he's a professional, so I recorded how he told the story and repeated it. In eight weeks we broke all the company records, and I made more money than ever before. It was literally overnight success—minus the ten years of personal development and honing my skills through trial, rejection, a couple of failed companies and many doubts along the way.

Looking back, though, I'm thankful for my trials. I experienced the value of true friendship and family and realized that my joy wasn't dependent upon cars, houses or the "things" of life. And in taking an honest look at myself, I see that I required some major humbling, compassion for others and experiencing the rawness of life for me to move to that next level of success, significance and growth. I don't believe the door could have opened for me as it has without my first being knocked down a few notches to put life in perspective.

In hitting rock bottom, I not only knew that I had nowhere else to go but up, I also knew I was building on a firm foundation. As we flew home from Philadelphia that day in October, I journalled about my experience. Even though my circumstances hadn't changed yet, my outlook had and I felt an inner peace. I was finally able to connect my challenges over the past years. I could now see the positive and how things had worked together to place me in that exact moment. I was, and still am, thankful for everything that has occurred.

Today, life has changed dramatically, but it's obviously not without its challenges. I've had many more lessons along the way and continue to realize that my life works best when I constantly push my comfort zone, continue growing in my faith and maintain a humble spirit to the best of my abilities.

About CJ Peterson

CJ Peterson was born and raised in Minnesota. He started business very early in life, waiting on customers at the age of five in his parents' Dairy Queen. The only wages he received were tips from customers, but the lessons of work ethic, customer service and honoring relationships that his parents provided paid off over the years.

CJ pursues life with a "take-charge, 150% enthusiasm, full-speed-ahead" attitude. When he was growing up, his parents never wanted to tell him that he could NOT do something, as that was like waving a red flag in front of a bull. They lived in mortal fear that he might want a swimming pool and that one day they would find a large hole in their backyard and all 32 neighborhood kids with shovels—digging. Thankfully, he instead directed his energy toward academics, athletics and business.

Even though CJ was a top student and athlete, he frequently got in trouble in school for selling things to his peers during class. His parents even got a call from the Booster Club because he was taking away business at the high school football games by collecting students' Dairy Queen orders and delivering them Friday night to the game.

CJ holds the second place record for all-time individual career wins in tennis at his high school, and he helped lead his team to a second-place state finish his junior year. He also finished third place and second place in state his junior and senior years, respectively, in individual doubles competition. After high school, he focused his energies on academics and athletic involvement at the University of Minnesota.

CJ quickly became one of the standout students at the U of M, constantly being chosen to meet with alumni to share his positive experience because of his involvement and passion. He was elected by his peers to be the Freshman Honors representative for the business school, and he helped turn the entrepreneurship club into the largest club on campus by recruiting more than 40 personal members and helping them spread the word. He was also the campaign manager as a freshman for Matt Clark, student body president, as they beat their nearest competitor by a 2-1 margin. CJ then became the facilities and housing representative, providing early input and support to the now on-campus football stadium. His involvement translated into a full scholarship from Carlson Companies for academics, leadership and extracurricular involvements.

Through the entrepreneurship club, he had the opportunity to meet and mentor with people like "Famous" Dave Anderson of Famous Dave's BBQ, Robert Stephens of the Geek Squad and Warren Nelson (Harvard MBA and multimillion-dollar earner) in the arena of network marketing.

Warren took CJ under his wing when CJ was 19 years old, encouraging him to read positive books and participate in leadership programs like Lifespring and Landmark Education. Upon CJ's graduation in 2003, Warren worked exclusively with him to help him build an international wellness business that spanned five countries, replaced a corporate income and made him the top producer under the age of 30 in the company. This experience, mentorship and success over the last seven years have led to CJ's greatest achievement to date in the network marketing arena with Independence Energy Alliance.

In eight weeks in Independence Energy Alliance, CJ and his business partner, Jon Gillardi, became the fastest-growing team and broke many company records. Today, CJ is one of four members on the advisory board providing counsel to the company and once again setting the pace for Generation X and Y builders.

CJ now lives in Irving, Texas. His future personal goals include breaking the million-dollar-a-year income level, running the Boston Marathon, qualifying for the Ironman World Championships in Kona, Hawaii, playing tennis at a competitive level again and becoming the best human being possible.

He finds his greatest fulfillment coaching people and consulting with companies to reach their highest potential, giving back to the community and growing in his faith daily.

CJ can be contacted through his website at www.CJPetersonInc.com, his Twitter page at www.twitter.com/CJPetersonInc, his Facebook fan page at www.facebook.com/CJPetersonInc, Skype @ CJPetersonInc, email at book@CJPetersonInc.com or by phone at (612) 467-9599.

Chapter 8

No Pain, No Gain
BY CARLOS ROGERS

"Arrange whatever pieces come your way."
- Virginia Woolf

As I return home from an amazing Cancun vacation, I sit here on the plane reminiscing about my life and feeling extremely blessed. I never would have imagined, coming from such humble beginnings, that I, Carlos A. Rogers, would enjoy the lifestyle that I do today. I'm living a life of freedom and purpose, and to think, it all came from a single phone call....

I was born to a single mother and raised in Birmingham, Alabama. My mom, a caring, loving, praying and God-fearing woman, was a hard-working and dedicated U.S. Postal Service employee. I saw my dad frequently, too, mostly on weekends and holidays.

In fact, it was at my dad's house that my love for sports was born. One of my fondest childhood memories is of playing football and basketball with my friends over at his place. Although most of my playmates towered over me, I wasn't scared of tackle football. I always thought, "The bigger they are, the harder they fall!"

One day, however, it was my turn to fall. I was hit and fell to the ground—hard. I heard a loud pop and felt excruciating pain throughout my seven-year-old body. I had broken my femur, the long leg bone between the hip and knee. You could actually see the bone jutting from my skin.

My screams of "Help me, Jesus!" were amplified by the wails of the ambulance siren, and the tears flowed, hot and stinging. I was immediately taken into surgery to repair the broken bone and then put into a body cast up to my navel. For three months I lay immobilized, with my leg suspended in a sling. Looking back, I'm sure I knew every TV show and commercial on the air during that time, because that's all I had to keep my mind occupied and off the pain.

I didn't know it then, but this experience would help prepare me for what was to come. What I did realize, even lying flat on my back at the young age of seven, was that you can't control what happens to you. You can control only your attitude and your reaction to the situation. Fortunately, I was mature for my age and able to stay positive. Having my good and faithful mom and grandma with me helped too.

There's no doubt that, for a young boy, giving up an entire summer was horrific. But I do believe that summer was a defining moment for me, and it helped me become more disciplined and appreciative. I realized then that I shouldn't take the body God gave me for granted. I knew that I had to be the best I could be with what I was blessed with.

About the age of 12, I started thinking creatively about how to make money. I would have my mom take me to Sweet Treats, a local store that sold candy in bulk at a discount. I'd then turn around and sell the candy at school for a profit. And the profits were significant: $50 to $100 a day was pretty good for a 12-year-old. Sometimes I'd surprise my mom and give her the money. In high school I used my profits to buy candy machines to place in local businesses.

I was always a hard worker and entrepreneurially minded. At 15, I started working at a barbecue joint called Costa's Barbecue seven miles from my house. My transportation system consisted of me pedaling my bike every morning to get there by 6:00. I worked as many hours as possible because I understood that there's nothing quite like having your own money. I even adopted a motto: "Short-term discomfort for long-term gains." During my time at the restaurant, I learned many skills that have continued to help me in life.

Like I said, I've always had a passion for sports, and I dreamed of some-day being a pro athlete. I continued to play football and basketball as I grew up, but I just couldn't seem to avoid injuries. In the seventh grade, I underwent surgery to remove a cyst and repair a torn cartilage in my right knee. "Here we go again, another wasted summer," I thought.

Once I recovered from the surgery, I naturally wanted to resume play-ing sports. My mom agreed, but encouraged me to choose just one. I guess she was worried that I wouldn't be able to excel at both basketball and football at the same time. So I chose basketball, since it had less contact and therefore less risk of injury. Mostly hustling, effort and skill, basketball came natural to me. I wasn't the most skilled or ath-letic player on the court, but knowing this only made me work twice as hard to keep up with the others. I always tried to give 110% effort, but I also realized that there is no "I" in "TEAM."

The odds always seemed to be against me, however. Throughout high school, I played out of position. I was a true point guard, but I played "2" guard—power forward. Since I was only six feet tall, this wasn't the best position for me. I didn't understand why my coach would play me there when he knew that I wanted to get a basketball scholarship and pursue my dream of being a pro athlete. His answer was that because only a small percentage of athletes actually get a scholarship, I should think of a more realistic career to aspire to. Now I've always had dream-stealers in my life, but I never thought my own coach would be one. How could he not encourage me to go after my dreams? I wasn't having that, so instead I became my own biggest fan.

I knew that you have to be confident in your own skills and abilities before someone else will be. Without confidence, you simply won't be effective. And there's an important difference between confidence and arrogance. People who don't understand this difference are often intimidated by confidence. The difference is this: Arrogant people think they are better than someone, and confident people know that no one is better than them. I always had confidence in my abilities, and I knew that I could play at the next level. And I proved it!

I received a basketball scholarship to Southern Union State Community College as a point guard, which was one of my goals. But, unbelievably, just a few weeks after signing for my scholarship, I broke the fifth metatarsal in my foot in a pickup game. Unsure of whether I'd be ready for the season, my college coach contemplated redshirting me that first year—exactly what I didn't want. I knew that now was my shot; I didn't want to wait another year.

I worked extremely hard to make a speedy recovery, so when it was time for practice to begin I was ready. I performed at a high level and ended up playing my first year. That year, we won state and came in sixth in the nation. All that hard work had paid off, and it felt great. But by my second year, though, I realized that I no longer wanted to play college ball. The pain and anguish of all of the injuries over the years had finally caught up with me, and my life-long dream of being a professional athlete ended.

I went on to receive my associate's degree, holding a respectable 3.9 GPA. But I realized that I was preparing myself to work for someone else, which wasn't what I wanted to do long-term.

After college, I went back to work at the barbeque joint, which gave me some time to think and sort things out. While I was deciding what I was going to do with my life, one day the comedian Ricky Smiley came through the drive-thru. He told me that "a man like me" should be in Hollywood on the big screen. Was I good-looking? Did he see some hidden acting ability in me? I didn't know, but I took his advice, and three months later I was headed to Los Angeles to seek fame and fortune. Within three weeks of my arrival there, I scored a minor role in *Beauty Shop*, the 2005 movie starring Queen Latifah, and I was on my way. Commercials and small television jobs followed, but I learned that being an up-and-coming actor meant you had to aggressively seek work and hustle, or else suffer with no income for long periods of time. As a starting actor, you get hired and fired the same day.

Remember that phone call at the beginning of my story? This is where it comes in. I was already looking for something that I could do on the side, at home, that didn't take a lot of time, and that could generate some serious residual income. I got a call about an opportunity with a home-based business from my friend Robbie that would change my life. Since he knew I was an entrepreneur with an open mind and looking to earn residual income, he thought it might be exactly what

I was looking for. I was very interested, and started reading self-help books like *Rich Dad, Poor Dad* and *The Business of the 21st Century* by Robert Kiyosaki and realized that, to get ahead in life, I needed to have leverage and build a network. I learned there are two ways to get ahead: One is to have people working with you, and the other is to have money working for you. Network marketing provides opportunities for both!

Today, I have a very successful business with several thousand partners who inspire and motivate each other on a daily basis. Now that I'm financially secure, I can sit back and look at my life somewhat philosophically. I work on my business as I see fit and take acting jobs when they come my way. The pressure of having to find acting jobs just to keep food on the table is now off, which is why I started my home-based business in the first place. I wanted to find acting jobs that allowed me to express the love I have for the art. Today, I'm a happy person because that's what I get to do. And while I love the lifestyle my business affords me, I do realize that money isn't everything. I see it merely as a tool to help me get the things I want.

As a result of starting and achieving success with my home-based business, I've been able to be in situations I would have never dreamed of. The freedom of owning your own life is a fantastic blessing, and I thank God for giving me a good mind and introducing me to the right people, as well as for my loving and praying mother, who has always been there for me and loved me unconditionally, and for my father, who instilled in me a great work ethic and taught me how to be a man.

One of my goals has always been to be able to help my mother. She sacrificed a lot for me in order to give me the lifestyle I had growing up, and I wanted to do the same thing for her. Recently, I was able to move her from Birmingham to Dallas, Texas, where she wanted to do ministry. I also took her to the Lexus dealership and told her to pick out a brand-new car, on me. Seeing the smile on her face was worth every ounce of pain I ever went through.

I tell people that sometimes you have to take two steps back to take a leap forward. When life hands you injuries, accept them and learn from them. Keep getting back up, stay positive, help others and learn all you can along the way. We can't always be that pro athlete, but we can have peace and joy in life—and really, isn't that the best thing anyway?

About Carlos Rogers

Carlos A. Rogers grew up in Birmingham, Alabama. When he left for college, he thought he was going to live his dream as an athlete. When he was plagued with injuries, he went to California to become an actor. Although he's not a well-known actor, he achieved success in network marketing. He has been the number one recruiter for his company, building an organization of several thousand product users and promoters.

Carlos is recognized internationally as a success and leadership trainer who educates and mentors others to achieve success in life. Carlos travels around the world helping others to live their dreams while he is fully living his dream.

You'll be sure to find Carlos somewhere on a vacation living life to the fullest!

Chapter 9

The Statue Within

BY LINDA NESBERG

"Every block of stone has a statue inside it, and it is the task of the sculptor to find it."

- Michelangelo

Similar to beautiful blocks of marble, people also have the potential to become whatever amazing works of art might be waiting inside, just beneath the surface. But this requires a sculptor and a chisel. What if *you* are the sculptor Michelangelo referred to in the quote above? What if your task in life is to find the strong, fearless statue inside? Would you have the courage to apply the chisel, in order to reveal the unseen statue of yourself?

I want to share with you how I discovered my own statue, deep inside. Here's my story...

I was born in rural Wisconsin in a town with a population of 506. My father was a cattle dealer and farmer, my mother a homemaker. By the time their ninth child, I, was born, my father's health and finances were plummeting because of his alcoholism. This left my mother to raise a total of fourteen children (ten boys and four girls). At his death, ten of us were under the age of 18. He left us little money, and we lost our home. Despite our plight, my mother tried to achieve a better reality for her family, and I am grateful for her enduring heart.

The Farm

My early life on the dairy farm holds fond memories of blue skies, fluffy clouds and warm sunshine. While we didn't have the luxury of toys or electronics, we were fortunate enough to have fields and haystacks. That may seem simple to modern children, but with our imaginations we created the best escapades our minds could conceive. I didn't know it at the time, but this imagination, this ability to create value from nothing, would later provide me with the tools I needed to chisel my dreams into reality and uncover the statue within me.

Since we didn't have toys, we had to entertain ourselves with what we did have—stuff around the farm. We would create homes from fallen leaves, piling them into stacks representing walls, rooms and hallways. Raking leaves was one of our daily chores, so we figured that we might as well design a home while we were at it! My brothers and I would play for hours in these makeshift abodes, adapting our creation with new rooms and doors.

The freshly laundered sheets that my mother hung on the clothesline became city streets, along which we strolled to chat with made-up neighbors and shop at the corner grocery store. Often we'd play hide and seek in the sheet-streets, peeking under the bottoms to catch a glimpse of a set of barefoot toes. Where were those boys now?!

Even to this day, I can recall the smell of those clean sheets, drying in the Wisconsin sunshine of my youth, signaling a simpler time, a time where we created something out of nothing.

Poverty

I didn't realize how destitute our family was becoming until I had been in elementary school a few years. There, I met other kids, who had better clothes and hygiene standards. When I was in the fifth grade, our family had no recourse but to apply for free school lunches because of our lack of income. Some days, that free meal was the only thing I ate that could be considered a proper meal.

I can think of only one definition of what it feels like to be poor—the notion that your family doesn't share an equal experience to those of the other families around you. The feeling of being poor is initially external, or it was for me in the fifth grade. By that, I mean it was mainly tied to the situations I experienced that showed me that I was poor. But it doesn't take long for that feeling to become internalized, which can shape how our statue is chiseled, as we move into the future with this feeling of being different from everyone else.

One summer I broke my leg, which deepened my understanding of just how poor our family was becoming. We were taking sacks of pig feed to a farm that we rented, and all of us kids were piled into the back of my dad's cattle truck, along with all the bags of feed. The truck's back door, which weighed about 200 pounds, was tied to its side door with binder twine from some old hay bales. We were traveling down our country road, and I was sitting in the corner. My brothers and I were dangling our feet out the back of the truck. Suddenly the wind snapped the twine and caught the door, causing it to swing around and smash right into me. My leg was crushed. I curled up in the corner, sobbing with the excruciating pain.

When we got to the farm I was set on the grass. My parents and brothers proceeded to unload the truck while I sat silently sobbing in the worst pain of my life. I remember my dad asking my mom what she was going to do with me. "I guess I will take her to the hospital," she said, very angry, glaring at me. And that is just what she did. She dropped me off and left, and I stayed overnight in the hospital by myself, with not one visitor. I never felt more alone in my entire life, and I was only seven years old. Mom and dad were so angry, because we had no insurance or money to pay for my hospital bills. I felt like such a burden to them. I was powerless to help my situation. I had no tools to fix the problem. I had no idea about my statue within.

I remember another time when I was about ten or eleven. A sister-in-law had come to help around the house shortly before my dad died. She cleaned the refrigerator so thoroughly that it sparkled. When I opened it later, I saw a gleaming white interior with one jug of bright orange Tang on the shelf. And there it was, the stark reality that all our family had in the refrigerator was a jug of Tang. There were very few dairy cows in the barn waiting to be milked, but inside there was not a drop of milk for any of the twelve us that were still living at home then. That external experience quickly internalized the feeling of being poor, of having nothing. A sense of determination was born deep inside of me that day. *This would not happen in my life ever again.* I would have more than Tang. I would chisel my own statue.

Lack of Father

My father was absent from my life in so many ways, mostly due to alcoholism. They say it is a spiritual, emotional and physical disease, and we felt those effects. I never, not even once, remember my father being home for dinner. After working every day, he frequented local taverns, which replaced the solace he should have received from coming home to his family. Sometimes he would bring home treats from the tavern—pretzels or small bags of penny candy. My brothers and I would delight in the small snacks. They probably symbolized the love he felt but couldn't give.

He passed away three months short of his forty-seventh birthday, his liver completely consumed with cirrhosis. I remember hearing that he had only an eighth of it left. There it was. He was gone physically from us. He died in January, a cold, barren month of the year in the Midwest. There was no father to protect me or to guide me, a small daughter. No lap to sit on, no affirmation of my value to come from a father's smile, the twinkle of his eye. No man to give that first love for a young girl to cherish, which sets the stage for all the men she will ever be involved with in her life. No father for a young man to ask for his daughter's hand in marriage. No father to walk her down the aisle at her wedding. No one with whom to dance the father–daughter dance at the reception. Nothing is left, except a cold, barren feeling, like the dreary winter day outside. The sculptor picks up her chisel.

The Turn: Track

Despite a childhood riddled with poverty and loss, and the fact that there appeared to be nothing to save me from the reality I found myself in, I chose not to permit my state to breathe into my being. Instead, I would question it.

In seventh grade, I had a wonderful teacher, Mr. Kinzinger, who challenged me in many ways. Once he asked the class, "How many of you think you will make one million dollars over your lifetime?" My hand shot straight up in the air, without a moment of hesitation. Knowing that my family lived in poverty, Mr. Kinzinger gave me a look of disbelief. "You think you will make a million dollars over your lifetime?" he asked. "Yes," I asserted, "One million dollars is not that much money." I was beginning to understand that I may have been given a block of stone, but if I had enough determination and the right chisel I could turn it into a work of art.

During physical education class the following spring, I was running the track during normal P.E. time. Mr. Graff, our history teacher, and one of the boys' track coaches watched as I ran. A little later they approached me, encouraging me to try out for track the following year. They thought I was a good runner. I'd never really been interested in track; heck, back then I didn't even know what the sport of track was all about. That was the first year that the sport was even open to girls.

Thinking back now, running was a skill I'd picked up chasing those ten brothers of mine around the fields and haystacks, back when we didn't have enough money for toys or electronics. (I still tease them that they were the reason I was so fast.)

The following year I entered high school. The coaches made sure I signed up for track, and off I went running. I never lost a meet until I got to the State track meet that year, where I finished in third place in two categories. I competed at the State meet each year of high school after that, too.

One of my coaches advised me that if I wanted to win gold I would have to do a little more than everyone else. He set me on a routine that I practiced every night throughout the season. In addition to doing the regular practices with the team (and then working a part-time job for two hours every day), I would return home and lace my track shoes up again. I would go onto the country road in front of our house and run sprints for 45 minutes in marked-off yards. Run, run, run. Run until I couldn't feel my legs any longer. The sculptor is chiseling.

This competition gave me new life. I will never forget the feeling of stepping onto the track. Digging my track shoes into the cinder, my eyes circling the full circumference of the track, knowing I was going to bust loose and take the lead in this race before the first corner, no matter what lane I had been assigned. On the back half, I knew I could ease into a stride that kept ahead of everyone else, and turn it on in the last quarter, knowing that the kick of the race had to be better than anyone else or I'd lose. The initial trick is getting out in front; after that the key is figuring out where the competition is and how to stay ahead of them. Listen for their footsteps, listen to their breath, move your arms faster, keep the lead, that's all that matters for the next 60 seconds. The statue is forming.

What I've Built

Competition was a character-building experience that propelled me into the rest of my life with all the tools I would need to shape my destiny, the statue within. Even when I lost a track meet, I gained the knowledge that at least I was a *competitor*. If I put my will and determination to task, I knew I would stay in the game. Once I knew that this drive to succeed was buried deep inside of me, I knew I had a chisel. I knew that it was up to me to form the statue within.

The Journey

When I was 22, newly married with a baby of 13 months, my mother succumbed to cancer. It was a grueling death that lasted three years. At this time, there were three children left at home under 18. As she lay dying in the hospital, full of cancer, she struggled with her life ending and leaving those three without a parent. I couldn't imagine this feeling, but I knew how heavy it was on her heart. I held her hand in the hospital and told her that it was time to leave this Earth, that those three kids would be taken care of by the rest of us. She shook her head no, and I assured her again and told her it was time to go home to her Father. I will never forget what happened. The absolute most peaceful look I have ever seen overcame her countenance, her wrinkled forehead erased itself of all lines, her body released, and she leaned back into her pillow, opened her eyes and smiled. She was ready.

My older sister took our two brothers ages 15 and 17, and I took our 12-year-old sister to raise. We both deeply loved those three children who were left. Chisel.

The Statue Within

With a few decades behind me, and hopefully a few more in front of me, the journey continues. I enjoy life with my husband of 33 years and our four children. I cherish every day that I have been blessed with their presence. I have achieved a six-figure income, own rental properties, and in recent years enjoy inspiring and motivating large groups. However, what I have learned along the way is much more valuable than any financial success. I have found ways to value the father I had, even if just for a short, brief period of my life.

The sculptor must take it all in, chisel away at the block of stone until the very soul of the stone is uncovered. The statue within is revealed. My statue is strong, beautiful and courageous. It is built on perseverance, hard work, a love of God and guidance from countless mentors in my life—some for a day, some for a much longer time.

I urge you to use the tools life hands you. You might not think your stone is beautiful or tools worthy, but give them a chance. Use what you've been given to chisel away, and discover your own statue that most surely lives within you.

About Linda Nesberg

Linda Nesberg grew up in a rural Wisconsin farming community. She is the ninth child of 14, with 10 of them being brothers. While growing up in poverty, she remained positive about her outlook on life and her ability to succeed.

Linda has worked in mid-level management for Fortune 100 companies and currently resides in Rochester, Minnesota. She is skilled in change management and leading organizations through difficult economic periods, bringing a positive spin to any situation.

She has been married for 33 years to her husband, David. They have raised four children and enjoy traveling with them and many other friends throughout the country.

She can be contacted at lindanesberg.net or lenesberg@gmail.com.

Chapter 10

I Qualify Myself

BY SHELLEY BLANZY

"I was once afraid of people saying, 'Who does she think she is?'
Now I have the courage to stand and say, 'This is who I am.'"

-Oprah Winfrey

One afternoon, a friend and I were ordering lunch at a local restaurant. I asked if the guacamole had onions, and the waitress said that, yes, it did. I don't like onions, so I asked her if the kitchen could make me some without onions. Glancing at my friend, I said jokingly to the waitress, "Tell them I'm a very important person, and ask if they'll please make me some guacamole without onions." When she returned from the kitchen, our waitress apologized, saying the guacamole was premade and that they were unable to remove the onions. Then she asked, "But I'm curious as to what qualifies you as so important?" I paused a moment, looked at my friend, and then said to her, "*I* qualify myself."

And that's been my basic philosophy throughout life. I've survived tragedy after tragedy and endured untold struggles and pain. I finally decided to "qualify myself" to live a life of fulfillment rather than suffering. What do I mean by "qualifying myself"? To qualify means "to be or make somebody suitable," "to have a skill or necessary attribute" or "to give somebody such a skill or attribute" or "to become legally eligible for a position or privilege." The synonyms for qualify include: be suitable, meet the requirements, be in the running, be eligible, make the grade, succeed, be licensed, be nominated and be certified.

You see, I had to decide *myself* that I was eligible for fulfillment and happiness because my life was so screwed up and full of chaos and abuse that there was literally no one else to do it for me. I had no one to pour into me or feed my soul, no one to point me in a positive direction. Anything good had to come from within, from my own innate drive and the God-given resolution deep inside.

Losing my father when I was only two made life incredibly difficult for my family. We lived on social security and welfare. We didn't have much more than just what it took to meet our basic needs. My mom went on to remarry a very verbally and physically abusive man. The awful memories of getting beat up, and watching it happen to those I loved, will forever be engrained in me. The pain and hurt in my mother's voice were terrifying as we sought shelter in the wee hours of the night. Sometimes, family or friends would take us in, but as in so many other domestic-violence situations, we too returned to the scene of the crime time and again.

As a child, I had no control over my circumstances; I could control only my thoughts. Even then, I knew the abusive lifestyle was wrong, though it wasn't uncommon in our neighborhood.

One of my earliest memories is of being taken to a barn and sexually molested by a family member at the age of five. This happened repeatedly. Not only did it hurt physically, but it left me with emotional scars, too. I had an overwhelming feeling of shame and betrayal. I was only a child, and yet even I knew it was wrong. No one "qualified" my rescue. So I qualified my *survival*.

At school, I lived the stereotypical embarrassment of being the "free lunch girl." And at the grocery store, we paid for the food with that pretty colored money, the colors of poverty. I knew when I grew up that I would not shop with that colored money. I would somehow have financial security and break free from the curse of poverty in my life. I would not allow my childhood circumstances to define my future. I would overcome the failures of my mother's life; I would succeed and give my own children a life that bore no resemblance to mine. My thoughts were my only consolation during these hard times.

As I grew up, I was taught to actually participate in unacceptable behaviors, like stealing. The food we didn't purchase was the meat that my mother couldn't afford to buy. I would watch as she'd shove the meat packages down the front of her pants. When we needed shoes, my mother would take us to the store, barefoot, and we would walk out with new shoes on. I didn't walk out of that store with the pride of my mother having bought me new shoes. No, instead I slunk out with the knowledge that the shoes on my feet were stolen. Remember when you were a kid and you got new shoes? Perhaps they made you feel as though you could run faster or jump higher? Mine made me afraid that the police would come and get me for stealing. We were the family of poverty and disgrace.

I dreaded the consequences that I knew had to come, and one day they did. I was so afraid. The police questioned me; they asked me if we had been stealing. They said if I told the truth, they wouldn't take my mom. So, I told the truth. I was as scared as I could be. I was so afraid they would take my mom from me. I needed her. Though life was a mess, I needed my mom. Thank God this was just a slap on the hand with little consequences. I had already lost my father.

I knew that there must be more out there—that safety had to exist… that loving people and relationships flourished somewhere. It was my hope and dream to find this place. I would sometimes stand in front of the mirror and cry out to my father, asking him why he left me to deal with all of this craziness. Hurt and abandoned, I was angry at a father I didn't know. I thought that perhaps if he'd been there, none of it would be happening.

Deep down, I knew there had to be more to life than the way we lived. So, until I could find it, I worked to be the best person that I could be, believing that one day life would be better. I thought that if I could be better and do better, I might someday be blessed with the "better life."

My saving grace was that even as a child, I was driven. I wanted more out of life, so I went after it. I started babysitting at nine. At the age of 11, I picked beans on a farm. From babysitting and bean picking, I went from working for others to working for myself. By the time I was 14, I was cutting hair. At 22, I owned my own hair salon. I wound up selling the salon, though, just before it became profitable. I got married and moved to another state to follow my dream of being a stay-at-home mom.

My dreams of motherhood and family security turned sour though—twice. My relationships always seemed to end in infidelity. The first time was when I found out that my high school sweetheart was with another girl while we were dating. Heartbroken, I turned my back on him and walked away. The pattern repeated when my first husband did the same thing. When I married the second time, it was with high hopes the pattern would finally be broken. But he too turned out like the others. I think I always knew in the back of my mind that he was cheating, but I held on, hoping it wasn't true. I thought that if I were just a good enough person, a good enough wife and mother, he'd stop. Finally, I asked God to confirm my fears. He did, and the beginning of the end of my marriage was put into place.

I tried to wrap my brain around the pain—this great pain of loss and self-defeat. Why was I not good enough for my man not to wander? What was so wrong with me that they had to cheat? When would it be my time to find a soft place to land? I always longed for a soul-mate who would love me for who I am on the inside, without feeling the need to "look elsewhere."

It's taken some time for me to understand that my partners' infidelity wasn't about me. I finally realized that it was about *them* and their lack of respect for themselves and for God. In a last-ditch effort to save my marriage, I encouraged my husband to build a business with me. It didn't work, but I did receive the grand blessing from God of allowing me to continue to build the business alone. As I did, I was further blessed through a self-development program that helped me to heal and taught me to use my pain to fuel my success. I'm proud to say that I now have a very large and growing business; and as a woman, mother and someone who's had to qualify her own life, my passion is to empower my children to qualify theirs. I try to live my life as a nonjudgmental, positive person, and I'm most fulfilled and happiest helping others. Now I can help people achieve their dreams while achieving my own goals and desires through my business.

As a woman, I also love to help empower other women. I understand how they can lose themselves to their circumstances, just like I almost did. We start caring for our spouse or significant other, our children, jobs and everyday responsibilities, and we tend to take a backseat in our own lives. But it doesn't have to be that way. We *can* live out our dreams while taking care of our families. Being in a network marketing business has been a great vehicle for me to inspire women to take control of their lives with style and elegance. I help them understand that they, too, can become who they were destined to be.

To look at me today, it might be difficult to imagine how hard I had to work to get to where I am. I look like the girl who was born with a silver spoon in her mouth. I wasn't—I just learned how to put one there and that's where I intend to keep it. My achievements in life resulted directly from my strategies for success, which I now teach to others. I've never allowed past circumstances to define me. *I define me.* I decide who I am.

I'm blessed that, growing up, I never identified with our lack of money or felt like my past predicted my future. My innate inner spirit always projected a vision of myself that was different from how others saw me. And while I've sometimes struggled with people thinking that I feel like I'm better than them, this is hardly the case—I'm no different from anyone else. The only distinction is that I have the ability to focus and maintain my vision despite the circumstances of my life. Many people judge me, seeing the polished woman I've become but not knowing what I've had to endure. It was my innate beliefs and morals that helped me survive my childhood, and a deliberate choice to read self-improvement books and attend seminars that helped me succeed in my adult life. Anyone who has the desire *can* achieve anything and everything they set out for.

God has blessed me immensely; he has strengthened me and allowed me to overcome all the obstacles and struggles in my life. But being strong doesn't mean you don't feel pain. In fact, pain has always been a worthy adversary; it makes me stronger. So I don't share my story of pain to elicit sympathy, but to encourage you to use your own pain to create hope, and to develop your own story of change and continual persistence.

I've realized that in life, God allows only what you can handle. And he won't give you what you desire until you align yourself with him. Once I understood this, I could truly qualify myself—a strong, powerful woman living a life of integrity, giving people hope and the belief that they can become anybody they want to be. Now I challenge you to qualify *yourself.* Don't let your pain or suffering stop you. Use the struggles in your life to grow and be the best that you can be.

About Shelley Blanzy

Shelley was originally born and raised in Toledo, Ohio, and currently lives in Chicago. With a passion for loving her family and empowering other people, she is a strong, powerful woman living a life of integrity. Shelley enjoys giving people hope and instilling in them the belief that they can become whoever they want to be.

Shelley has owned and operated multiple businesses for several years. She found her calling when she was introduced to network marketing while raising her children. She has become one of the most sought-after trainers in the company and has built several successful sales organizations around the country.

Shelley speaks, trains and inspires people all over the world. She currently is leading the expansion of one of the fastest growing Internet-based travel companies in the world.

In her personal life, Shelley strives to set an example for her kids, living an authentic life of honesty and integrity. She also has a passion for helping other women live their dreams by balancing the roles of business owner and single mother.

Chapter 11

A Hard Life

BY AJAYÉ CARTER

"A winner knows when to swallow his/her pride in order to resolve a higher cause or purpose. Winners also understand that it is impossible to win by themselves."

- Johnny Wimbrey

I grew up in South Central Los Angeles in the 1960s and 70s. It wasn't easy for a young black kid. Societal statistics would probably reveal that a black male raised in South Central Los Angeles in a single-family home would most likely capitulate to society norms—possibly floating in and out of jail, maybe strung out on drugs, conceivably not even living much past the age of 18. I beat the odds.

My parents split when I was young. Since I was forced to face life as a young man without a father's daily guidance and direction, I looked to the streets and the norms of the society surrounding me to survive. All

I ever wanted or needed was my father, but he wasn't there. The ache inside me was deep.

My mother, sister and I survived on just my mom's salary. She wore the same clothes to work three times a week, but she made sure they were washed and ironed every day. To save on the cost of school clothes, my mom enrolled us in a Catholic elementary school—kids at that school wore a uniform instead of regular street clothes. I also remember wearing PF Flyers tennis shoes in the late 60s. I got one pair every two years. As they got smaller on my ever-growing feet, I would purposely try to wear a hole in them, hoping to get a new pair like other kids in the neighborhood.

But my mom knew how to make her meager budget stretch. She had me trace the outline of my foot on a cardboard box, which she then cut out for me to place inside the shoe, creating a makeshift new sole, which I was very careful to make sure no one ever saw.

The tennis shoes I wore as a kid

We didn't have much, but we got by. I remember being laughed at and teased growing up because my mother would iron patches on my holey jeans. I loved sports and played hard, so my jeans took quite a beating.

Because we often didn't have the money in December, the Carter household would celebrate Christmas in January, or even sometimes in February.

Because my father was not a major part of my youth, my mom kept me involved in boys' camps, Cub Scouts and sports. I began little league baseball at the age of eight and continued to enjoy sports into high school.

Life for a kid in my situation wasn't very easy. I was bullied in elementary school, and ran home from school many days to avoid confrontations. The neighborhood crew, a gang of kids and neighbors, would see me running. They would shout at me, "You can't run scared all your life!"

One day I ran home in fear of a bully who wanted to beat me up. The next day, the neighborhood kids surrounded me and demanded that I point the bully out to them. I was scared and started to cry. They told the bully that I wanted to fight him.

I tried to run away but the crowd shoved me back into the center of the ring, and I was forced to fight. Terror enveloped me as the bully charged; I truly feared for my life. I started to swing—and somehow I kept on swinging until I finally felt myself being pulled from him.

Coming out of my frenzied state after the fight, I heard the crowd cheering and felt my heart pounding as he lay there, knots covering his face. A sense of relief washed over me as I realized that I would never again have to be afraid of him. I never backed down from another confrontation and gained notoriety as a good fighter.

The neighborhood crew became my big brothers and protectors. In exchange for their brotherhood, I was expected to do certain things. They would approach me with requests like, "I want you to fight John Lee," or "You need to take care of little Darrell." By the time I reached high school, I'd developed a reputation—and it wasn't a good one. I never turned down a dare or a fight, and as a result, in the 10th grade, I was kicked out of the all-boys Catholic high school and transferred across town to Los Angeles High School.

Old Habits Die Hard

At the new school, I made the starting lineup, having beat out the previous year's starter. But getting acclimated to a public school after the all-boys Catholic school proved to be quite a culture shock. My grades suffered, falling to a C or D average at best. At 15, I began to experiment with alcohol as a way to escape the pain of a tough childhood. In addition, largely to be accepted in a society ruled by violence, drugs and alcohol, I once again sought the brotherhood of a gang.

The gang I joined prevented trouble by any means necessary, but it didn't necessarily look for trouble, for which I remain grateful to this day.

I graduated Los Angeles High School in 1974. Graduation felt like a load of bricks had been lifted from my shoulders but deciding what to do next was a challenge. I eventually followed the lead of my childhood best friend, Lawrence Garrett, and applied to West Los Angeles College, where former NFL quarterback Harold "Warren" Moon had played football in his early years.

Lessons Learned as a Young Adult

Unfortunately, in college as in high school, I chose not to take my studies seriously. I didn't maintain the NCAA eligibility requirement of a 2.0 grade point average. I left home early every morning but didn't go to class. I simply hung out day after day, gradually giving myself over to alcohol and drugs.

One particularly sunny LA morning, two of my old high school buddies and I strolled down Pico Boulevard, under the influence even at that early hour, and came to an Armed Forces Recruitment Station. Looking back, I truly believe God was watching over us and that He intervened on our behalf. We all looked at each other, laughed out loud and sauntered into the recruiting station, more as a joke than anything else. We took the military entrance exam, and a few weeks later we each received a letter from the Department of the Navy informing us that we had passed! We were so surprised by the realization that, with little or no effort, we had actually accomplished something.

I called my mother and told her I'd passed the Navy exam. I asked her what I should do. After a long pause, she simply said, "Son, that is one question you will have to answer on your own," and then she hung up. I can still hear that loud 1970s dial tone. I looked at the phone, stunned. So, just as I had followed the lead of my childhood best friend and enrolled in college, my high school friends followed my lead. On December 28, 1976, we all joined the Navy in the Buddy Enlistment Program.

Big Brothers in the Navy

After boot camp, my first duty station was the aircraft carrier USS Kitty Hawk. Because I hadn't scored high enough on the military entrance exam, I didn't qualify for a specific career occupation. I went to an apprentice school where any and all blue-collar jobs are performed (painting, chipping, sanding, tying knots, rigging equipment, etc.).

As in my youth, I didn't realize until later how valuable the lessons I learned in the Navy would prove to be. For example, in 1978, I was told by my supervisor, "As long as you work for me, you will never go any higher than this." He held his hand at chest level, about four feet in the air, indicating mediocrity. Flabbergasted, I asked him to repeat himself; I wasn't sure I'd heard him correctly. He said it again, and my mind snapped to my own defense. I said to myself, "This man must not know who I am. I am from South Central LA. He must be a racist!"

For the next two years, even though I did my job, I did not advance. My frustrated response was to become rebellious, defiant and very resistant to authority. After a few outbursts, I was approached by two sailors, Elliot Simpson and Clarence Peters, whom today we would call "mentors" and to whom I'll always be grateful. These good men decided they had seen enough of my belligerent behavior and they took me under their wings and began to mentor and coach me. They taught me a lesson I've always held onto: Never use discrimination as an excuse for your own lack of self-development. That was the best advice I ever received during those tough times.

With two more "big brothers" looking after me, I charted a new direction for my career and gained a bit more confidence, stability and job security.

In 1986 my mother passed away, and my sister and I inherited her life insurance money as well as proceeds from the sale of her home. You would think that suddenly getting a windfall of cash would be a blessing, but I was unsure of how to proceed. Having grown up with little to spare, and no father available to answer questions or offer sound advice, I was lacking in experience and sound judgment in this area. I had my mother's brand-new Mercedes Benz decked out with an AMG kit, chrome wheels, TV, telephone and dark tinted windows. My look was topped off with my own "Mr. T starter kit," complete with multiple gold chains, watches and rings. I was often seen by my Navy peers and superiors rolling back and forth between San Diego and Los Angeles. I can only imagine what they must have thought.

Over the next decade, I remained in the same pay grade while many people whom I'd trained passed me up as they climbed the promotion ladder. I had all the necessary qualifications for advancement, but for some reason I wasn't being promoted to Chief Petty Officer. During this time, the Navy's policy was that if you didn't make the rank of E-7 (Chief Petty Officer) within 20 years, you'd be discharged.

In 1993, I lost a teammate, a man just 26 years old who was recently married and had a six-year-old son. He died as I watched four trauma teams trying to revive him over a three-hour period. I was 37 years old at the time, and I believed it should have been me instead of him because he was so young. I entered alcohol rehab, and on July 3, 1993, had my last drink.

Figuring Out What's Really Important

I returned from being stationed overseas and immediately began to focus on changing the people around me. I enrolled in Southern Illinois University and completed three years of college, but I wasn't able to achieve my degree because of not passing certain classes back in high school.

In 1994, I became certified as a civil rights trainer/investigator and program manager. Training and education became my passion. After attending Alcoholics Anonymous meetings and many hours of counseling sessions, I began to focus on myself—I finally felt that I had a purpose, and I asked God to be the head of my life and to guide me.

I began to ponder questions like these:

1. If you had one opportunity to change anything in your life that would lead you to accomplish your dreams and goals, what would that change be?

2. What is the number one reason most people don't step out of their comfort zone to reach toward greatness? I've come to believe that it's simply fear of the unknown.

Life Lessons Learned Late

I never achieved the rank of E7 in the Navy, and so in January 1997, I retired under honorable conditions after 20 years of service. After retiring, I happened across a former shipmate one day who wanted to know whom I'd pissed off in the Navy. "What do you mean?" I demanded, very curious. He told me that at his job on the Chief Selection Board at Navy Headquarters he'd overheard a conversation about how my service record had been flagged "pending investigation."

I learned that I'd been under investigation for possible involvement with drugs. Immediately, I began to recall the many times that I'd come through the front gate on base and been stopped for inspection (complete with drug-sniffing dogs) at least three or four times a week. No wonder I'd constantly been asked about my whereabouts and what I was doing that weekend.

I realized my image had been causing a setback on my professional growth. A 30-year-old sailor, with a Mercedes Benz, a second car, and two houses, must be selling drugs. That day I realized that a person's image is more important that their reputation. Specifically, I realized that how you are perceived by others, rather than how you see yourself, is what will determine your level of success.

I began the process of self-education in order to develop as a speaker. I have invested in training CDs and turned my car into a "drive-time university." I've surrounded myself with individuals who are successful in the public speaking arena. I've attended multiple motivational seminars. You don't have to have a degree, you just need desire.

Over the past four years, my salary has grown from five to six figures. I don't share this to impress anyone, but rather to impress upon you that, against all odds, it is still possible to reach your goals and dreams.

The margin of error in sports like Nascar, track and field, etc., can be measured in milliseconds. The difference between 211° F and 212° F is obviously one degree. When you examine it closely, you realize that at 211 degrees, water is hot, but at 212 degrees water begins to boil, creating steam, which is so powerful it can propel a locomotive down the train tracks. You can learn more and take the 212-degree challenge at www.ajayecarter.com.

I would like to dedicate this chapter to a mentor of mine who recently was called home, the late Keith Harrell.

About Ajayé Carter

Ajayé Carter has 20 years of experience of technical management and business practices in the administration of an Equal Employment Opportunity (EEO) program. He has an in-depth knowledge of federal sector EEO laws, directives and executive orders. A recognized EEO subject matter expert responsible for executive leadership, policy and direction, Ajayé oversees the Affirmative Employment, Diversity and EEO Complaints programs affecting employee equal employment opportunities at four district offices located in Fort Worth and Galveston, Texas; Tulsa, Oklahoma, and Little Rock, Arkansas. He has served the majority of his federal career in the capacity of an EEO Complaints Manager at the field, district, major command and headquarter levels for various government agencies.

A well-known master facilitator who has a unique ability to entertain, educate and involve audience members in his powerful interactive presentations, Ajayé specializes in bringing together intellectual differences in individuals and motivating them to work together. By effectively employing these skills, he has helped organizations maintain the highest degree of readiness by fostering positive human relations interaction throughout a diverse workforce.

By building bridges between cultures and experiences, Ajayé brings insight to his audiences via seminars, workshops and focus groups to empower individuals in organizations to create and control their own vision and destination in their personal and professional lives. An advocate of "community," Ajayé is a former member and mentor of Big Brothers/Big Sisters of America and the Virginia Department of Juvenile Justice Court for first-time offenders. Founder and former President of Building Bridges of Understanding, a Center of Excellence for Equal Employment Opportunity, and now the President and Chief Executive Office of Career Image Consultants, Mentoring Tomorrow's Leaders in the 21st Century, Ajayé is a truly dedicated professional.

Ajayé is a native of Los Angeles California; a retired, decorated Navy veteran of 20 years; a graduate of the Department of Defense, Equal Opportunity Management Institute; and a graduate of the Army's Management Staff College: Continuing Education for Senior Leaders, Advanced Leadership, Organizational Leadership and Personnel Management for Executives programs. In addition, he is a certified Equal Employment Opportunity Commission (EEOC), Advanced Conflict Mediator.

Chapter 12

Destined for Success

BY MARGARITA KILILI

"Your beliefs become your thoughts, your thoughts become your words, your words become your actions, your actions become your habits, your habits become your values, your values become your destiny."

- Mahatma Gandhi

I've had big dreams my whole life long. I believe in living a life by design and I love having choices. I've learned to make the most out of anything that comes my way—including obstacles. I'm actually grateful for the obstacles I've encountered, because through them I've learned that I can't always control what happens in everyday situations. But rather than allowing obstacles to block my dreams, thankfully I realized early on that there is always a way around them. I've learned to embrace life's challenges because they not only strengthen my desire to achieve my dreams, they also help me to grow as a person.

I'm now 35 years old and thankful that I pursued my dreams. I'm married to my soul mate, we've traveled to more than 20 countries so far, I'm the proud mother of two wonderful "treasures" as I call them, we live in our dream house, we have a wonderful network of friends, and I'm a successful speech–language pathologist, which is what I always wanted to do. I always believed I was destined to help people; to help them trust in their own abilities, to help them overcome their limitations and to help them thrive. I've been able to do that with my clients during the past decade, but over the last couple of years, an opportunity has come my way to expand my horizons beyond the field of speech–language therapy. Today, I show people how to design their lives on their own terms, how to create choices in their lives and overcome their obstacles. I show them how to pursue their dreams just like I did. The secret lies in the realization that everything is a matter of mindset. If you focus on your problems, more will come your way. If you focus on solutions, opportunities will appear around you.

I am so grateful to have been born into a loving and supportive family on the small island of Cyprus. My parents are my heroes, and my brother and sister are so deeply inside my heart that they are truly a part of my character. A dear cousin, Andria, is my inspiration, and I believe that I owe everything I am today to her, even though she was younger than me. She was born hard of hearing, to the point that she was classified as deaf by her doctors. But she didn't let that define her. She was so energetic, fun, loving and strong—and had such a dominant personality—that she lived a life of success and triumph despite her handicap. She was a tennis champion in Cyprus; in fact, before the age of 18, she played in the professional championship for girls and for women. That was unheard of for someone with her "disability." How did she do that? Quite simply, she had unbridled passion and she practiced her game over and over again, tirelessly, until she mastered it. She allowed herself no excuses, which would have been the easiest thing to do, considering her condition. She even studied dance abroad. She didn't let anybody steal her dreams, which was an incredible lesson for me. She's the reason I wanted to become a speech–language therapist and to make communication between people my life-long mission. She made me believe that I would achieve whatever I set my mind and my heart on.

Tragically, Andria passed on unexpectedly at age 20, just months before we were planning to tour the U.S. for her twenty-first birthday. All my hopes came crashing down, and my whole family was devastated. The "why" was unbearable, and I felt helpless. To help cope with the pain, my aunt and I started reading books about the meaning of life, life after death, and personal growth. This opened a whole new world for me, which allowed me to regain faith in myself and to think about the legacy I wanted to leave when I was gone. I made a promise to myself that, just like Andria, I would never settle for the ordinary, the norm or the expected. Instead, I would shoot for my dreams and make no compromises.

Along the path to achieving my dreams, I've made a few discoveries. I've learned that we all have limiting beliefs about ourselves, which hold us back from achieving the aspirations we had when we were younger. These limiting beliefs are usually subconscious. They're based on our past and are rooted in our fears and failures. They become our "disabilities." And unless we focus on *designing* our future, these beliefs can build obstacles around us that prevent us from taking action. To avoid this kind of "paralysis," we must build our skills by making small, positive changes that guide us in the right direction every day. Once we determine what's important in life and decide to fight for that dream, we're ready to take the first step. One thing that kept me in the fight was my conscious choice to be around positive people and to participate in personal-development seminars. I can't describe how much this stoked my desire for achieving my dreams and goals and kept it burning strong.

But I doubt I'd be where I am today if I hadn't also experienced some personal challenges. Quite simply, I was a loner growing up. One of my earliest memories is of being around three years old, all alone, playing in my grandmother's basement with some everyday, household items. I had the best toys at home, but I preferred to use my imagination. Once in kindergarten, I didn't talk to anybody, played on my own and rarely made eye contact. I had poor social skills, but deep down inside I was happy. I was comfortable in my solitary world, whereas talking and playing with other children made me nervous. I never knew what to say and never asked any questions. I stayed in my comfort zone for a long time; in fact by today's standards, I could easily have been classified as "selectively mute."

As I got a little older, a desire for friends began to grow in me, but I just didn't know how to approach anyone. I was smart, and over time I became good at observing what other children talked about and how they played, so my stress level around them went down a notch. Now I use that strategy all the time. I try to model someone who's already successful in what I want to improve, and I build my skills one at a time. Back then, I began to realize that having friends could be fun for me too, but I wasn't ready yet to take a leap of faith and talk to someone. I had an enormous fear of failure and very low self-esteem. Why would anyone care about what I had to say? I was too afraid of rejection.

One day, the school principal came into the classroom and had me sing in front of the whole class. I was terrified, but I was more scared to tell him no, so I did it. That was my turning point. I sang with all my heart, and the whole class looked at me in amazement. I was in the spotlight for the first time—and I loved it. I was outside of my comfort zone and now well on my way to the next level.

From then until now, every time I face a fear, I have success. I realized that *the only way to overcome an obstacle is to stop looking at it* and instead to look *beyond* it, to visualize the end result and take massive action toward that vision. Then that same obstacle magically shrinks, and before you know it, you look back and laugh at how it made you feel. Mahatma Gandhi said, "Your beliefs become your thoughts, your thoughts become your words, your words become your actions, your actions become your habits, your habits become your values, your values become your destiny." So why believe that you *can't* do something and be destined for failure, when you can believe that you CAN and be destined for SUCCESS?

Thanks to my parents' sacrifices, I was blessed to attend a good private high school, and it was a safe ground to finally practice my social skills. I graduated in the top of my class, had a couple of social butterflies as best friends and was finally feeling included and important. My dream was to study abroad, but my parents couldn't afford it. I remember my dad bringing me job applications from a bank, which was considered a safe, secure job on the island. But I tore it up each time, hurting his feelings. I was stubborn and wouldn't compromise. My dream was so big, I would not settle, not even for a secure job. I preferred to take a low-paying temporary job to save some money, and I applied for a scholarship to study in the U.S.

I had a lot of potential to get that scholarship, and I knew it was my only shot. But I was scared. All I could focus on was my fear that, if I didn't get that scholarship, I would be stuck in a future that I did not dream about. I was more focused on my fear of loss than on the potential achievement, and in the interview for the scholarship I was really nervous. All I could think about was, "Don't mess this up; this is your only chance." Guess what? I was rejected and devastated to say the least.

I could have easily given up and filled out that bank job application, but I knew that I would not be happy doing that for the rest of my life. So I decided instead to reject my past failure, and I applied again the next year for the same scholarship. This time, I went in with the attitude that I had nothing to lose, so I was not even nervous. I focused on my dream and I was excited. I just shared my dreams and no longer feared that anyone had the power to stop them. I knew already I would find a way to reach them, even if I was rejected again. This shift in my psychology brought out my passion and enthusiasm. I still remember my family's amazement when I opened the letter awarding me a full scholarship and opening the doors to realizing my dream. Nothing had changed on my application; my grades and test scores were the same. Everything was the same, except my attitude. I went into the interview with a mindset, a posture, that I knew exactly what I wanted and I would somehow find a way to get it. I spent seven amazing years studying and traveling in the U.S., and the experiences and the memories were priceless. But I would not have them right now if I hadn't changed my attitude back then.

Posture is incredibly empowering, and everyone who isn't at the point they want to be in any part of their life is probably missing that link. Because of my posture, I was able to travel and study in the United States for the next seven years, mastering my social skills with diverse and interesting people. That cultural shock made me finally grow out of what others used to consider my worst weakness. If you want to get posture in your life, you need faith in your vision and in yourself. You need to stop feeling sorry over whatever happened in your past and for whatever you can't do yet, and finally stop making excuses for yourself. One of my favorite quotes is "Too many of us are not living our dreams because we are living our fears," by Les Brown. It's up to us to change that.

I used to think I couldn't change my character until I heard Anthony

Robbins say "Your past does not equal your future," and "A real decision is measured by the fact that you've taken a new action. If there's no action, you haven't truly decided." It dawned on me that I was not to let my past define who I wanted to be. I would not let my "baggage" hold me down. I was free to make a decision, a new beginning, with new goals and a new direction. My past failures were my lessons. From now on, I would no longer be a "victim" of circumstances but a "creator" of circumstances. Not only was this new resource of personal development through books, audios and videos empowering me, it was shaping a whole new world for me. Emotionally, personal development helped me get closure in everything that had hurt me in the past. My stress level went down, and I became grateful and happier. There are too many angry and depressed people in the world wasting valuable time focusing on all the negativity in their lives. Just imagine: They could be focusing on their dreams and making miracles happen for themselves. Don't let that be you.

I believe that each person has a gift or a talent, something they're good at. But society often labels us based on what we *can't* do. There's a tendency toward criticism in the world, and we as humans usually believe in others' perceptions of ourselves. The key to unlocking that calling, that passion, and to realizing every goal you have is to have immense desire and to embark on a journey of personal development. If I hadn't started reading books, attending regular personal-development seminars, watching videos and listening to audios in my car, I would probably still be a person with a social disability, judged by society's standards.

What have you achieved in life so far? What are you successful at right now? What do you want to have? How badly do you want it? What can you do today to change the direction you're going? One of my mentors, Jim Rohn, said, "The same wind blows on us all. It is the set of the sails, not the direction of the wind, that determines which way we will go."

I urge you not procrastinate in making your dreams come true. It only takes one step at a time. But every minute that goes without action is another day wasted. Just make a decision, make a small change in the right direction and make that positive change a habit. Be committed to your goal and take massive action. The end result will come faster than you think.

About Margarita Kilili

Margarita Kilili grew up on the island of Cyprus and was granted a full scholarship for study in the U.S. by the Fulbright Organization. She holds a Bachelor's degree with a double major in Psychology and Communicative Disorders/Speech-Language Pathology (SLP) from the University of Wisconsin–Madison. She graduated with a Master's degree in 2002 from San Diego State University as a Speech-Language Pathologist (SLP) and was employed for one year by the San Diego Unified School District. She returned to Cyprus in 2004, married and had two children. Now with her own private practice for speech-language therapy with adults and children, she focuses on a caseload with children under the autism spectrum. She served on the board for the Association of Registered SLPs in Cyprus and has attended numerous continuing-education seminars in the field. She is currently an SLP in the public schools in Cyprus. Since 2010 she has been part of an organization that allows her to travel the world and inspire others to improve their lives and live their dreams.

Website: http://margaritakilili.com/
Email: mgkilili@hotmail.com
Facebook: http://www.facebook.com/mgkilili

Chapter 13

The Journey

BY JAMES LEE

*"There are two mistakes one can make along the road to truth...
not going all the way, and not starting."*

- Buddha

If someone were to ask you, "How's life?" what would your answer be?

Life is just a plain life if you aren't passionate about it, and if you aren't positive or excited about it. You might just call it—"life." And when you *are* passionate and excited about it, when you do ascribe great meaning to it, then suddenly life is no longer just a plain life. Now it's a *journey*.

And if life is a journey, then we've got to plan it, to know where we are starting from and how we want it to look at the end. Just like writing this chapter, I've got to draft out a plan to write it. To be honest, I'm scared, nervous and a little worried about the outcome of it. This is my very first time writing a chapter that is going to be part of an incredible book with great content featuring many established individuals with vast amounts of experiences in their own right. Will I be able to deliver my message in my chapter? Will people be able to accept what I write and to understand my point? I have a lot of questions, doubts and uncertainties about this part of my journey, as I began to write my first chapter. But if I allow blockages and doubts to keep me stuck, I will never get started. So, I told myself, whatever the outcome may be, just get started!

So here goes! I am delivering my chapter with six parts. They are meant to give you a clear breakdown of how I work on my journey, and they may apply to anyone who wants to plan his or her journey as well.

Six parts to a fulfilling journey:

1. The Starting Point
2. Plan the Route
3. Find Good Mentor(s)
4. Pay Attention
5. Get Excited About the Journey
6. Never Give Up the Journey

One | The Starting Point

In every journey there's always a starting point; so identifying where you're starting from is critical. Are you in a position where you *need* to start moving? Or are you already content in your own comfort zone, with no reason to move? If so, you may see no need to even begin on a journey.

But there's no reason that someone has to be unhappy about their current situation before they want a transformation. The decision to transform and begin a journey could simply be the desire to be or do better, or just to have a change of environment from the status quo.

Most people want a better life and desire to achieve more, but the irony is that often these same people hate uncertainty and resist change. That's why knowing where you're starting from is so important; it can motivate you to embrace the need to change and then actually begin your journey.

You may see your current job, relationship, spiritual well-being, financial status, physical health or something else as your own personal starting point. Once you identify it, and decide to begin the transformation, that's when your journey begins.

But sometimes, identifying your starting point can be daunting and scary. It's like investigating your own life. Most people are unprepared and unwilling to know where they currently stand. My own wakeup call came when I was 27. I was presented this "time check of life," and I'd like to share it with you now.

Warning: This information is disturbing to some people, and it may break you down—or wake you up. Calculations are based on an average life expectancy of 75 years of age.

Years of Age	Used (in Days)	Remaining (in Days)	Used (in Hours)	Remaining (in Hours)
0	0	27375	0	657000
5	1825	25550	43800	613200
10	3650	23725	87600	569400
15	5475	21900	131400	525600
20	7300	20075	175200	481800
25	9125	18250	219000	438000
30	10950	16425	262800	394200
35	12775	14600	306600	350400
40	14600	12775	350400	306600
45	16425	10950	394200	262800
50	18250	9125	438000	219000
55	20075	7300	481800	175200
60	21900	5475	525600	131400
65	23725	3650	569400	87600
70	25550	1825	613200	43800
75	27375	0	657000	0

And looking at this table yearly, or even daily, can be even more alarming.

When I saw this information, a couple of big questions immediately leaped out at me: "Where am I now?" and "What have I achieved?" That was when I realized that my days are numbered. It was time for me to take stock of my life and begin a true journey instead of just living. I told myself to make each day count and not waste it because I can't stop time or turn it back—no one can. I decided to start my journey right then, at age 27.

Two | Plan the Route

Once you decide to start your journey, you need a route or a path that you will take. It would be insane to go on a trip or drive somewhere without first planning the route. Without a plan, it could take quite a long time to get to your destination. In some cases, you might not even get there at all.

Have you ever wanted to get somewhere, whether by car or even just walking, without planning the route first—even if it's just consulting a mental map of the best way to get there? No, in your mind you picture the shortest, safest, easiest route before you set off. The same logic applies in planning the route for your life's journey. Think about what you will need, what skills will be helpful, and what ultimate goals you want to accomplish. Careful thought and planning are critical to an enjoyable journey and the most fulfilling outcome. Many people even find it helpful to write down their short- and long-term goals, and to refer to them at least once a week.

Three | Find Good Mentor(s)

We all know that if you want to master a skill, you need to first be taught that skill and then you must practice it. And we've all heard that practice makes perfect. But, as a mentor once told me, *practice alone will never make perfect if you've done it all wrong in the first place.* He said, "*Perfect* practice makes perfect." But how can you practice perfectly from the beginning? First, you need to find a mentor who's good at that skill and learn the skills from him or her. Then go and practice them.

Many people have that "I know it already" mentality, which is the worst attitude to have. Because once a cup is full, it's full; you can't fill it up anymore. I've learned that if you want to achieve greater heights and attain a higher skill set, always have the "Empty your cup" mind-set. Have a constant eagerness to learn. Be a humble student ready to take in information and skills from others. With this attitude, you will be able to find the right mentor who can and will impart the right skills and help you collapse the time frame for achieving success.

If planning the route is like drawing out a map to your destination, then finding a mentor is like looking for a tour guide or an explorer who has already been where you want to go. It will save you lots of time and help you reach your destination much more quickly.

Four | Pay Attention

Paying attention to what you do, how you learn and where you are headed is important. If you don't stay focused, you will easily be distracted and won't be able to stay on track with your plan. Your destination will keep changing, and that feeling of "lost in life" will creep in eventually.

It is not easy for anyone to stay 100% focused and pay attention all the time. One of the best ways to keep yourself on track and not deviate too much off course is to make sure you have someone and something to hold you accountable for your actions. One very effective way to hold yourself accountable is to find your reason WHY you want what you want. Identify what your dreams are and the ultimate reason why you chose this journey.

You simply can't focus or pay attention if what you want isn't clear in your mind from the beginning. If this is something that you have never really spent time thinking about, do commit yourself to do it soon. The sooner you have a clear mind on what you want and dig in to your WHY, the sooner you will be able to pay attention to the things and events going on around you that will help you find the right path. That's when the joy and fun begins.

Five | Get Excited About the Journey

Think about it: A journey is truly a journey when it's not just about you alone. A true journey is one in which you get to see and experience other people, objects, surroundings, scenery, events and cultures. These add life and vitality to your journey, and make it uniquely yours. A true journey can be compared to taking a vacation. Aren't you excited about your vacation the day (or sometimes even days, weeks or months) before you go on it? If you can tap into that same excitement as you begin your life journey, you will have a great experience walking through it, and it will be the time of your life.

When you are enthusiastic about your journey, your life will stay positive and attract positive energy into it as you stay on course. It's practically impossible to bring dull, boring, negativity into your journey if you stay excited.

Try smiling or laughing and feeling sad and down at the same time. You just can't do it, at least not for very long. You have a choice to be positive and excited about your journey, just as you have a choice about how you want your life to look. If you want to attract good stuff into your life, you have to stay excited about it all the time.

"Whatever you focus on will expand." This simple statement has become one of my biggest guiding principles in life for staying positive. Focus on what you want instead of what you don't want. The universe will bring you what you focus on.

Six | Never Give Up the Journey

As the saying goes, "Life is like a journey." If you give up on the journey, then you give up on life as well. Everyone deserves to have the life they set out for themselves. If you have a plan to make it good, it *will* be good. Life is good, and you *will* have a good life if you continue the journey without stopping. The only time when you stop walking this journey is when it's time for you to return to the divine place. Always believe that your life will get better and better because you are constantly walking the journey.

None of us knows when our success will come or when we will attain our dreams. But there is one sure way to know that you will never get there, and that's by giving up on it.

Here's a poem I use to help keep me going every time.

Don't Quit!

When things go wrong, as they sometimes will,
When the road you're trudging seems all uphill,
When the funds are low and the debts are high,
And you want to smile, but you have to sigh,
When care is pressing you down a bit,
Rest, if you must, but don't you quit.

Life is queer with its twists and turns,
As every one of us sometimes learns,
And many a failure turns about,
When he might have won had he stuck it out;
Don't give up though the pace seems slow—
You may succeed with another blow.

Often the goal is nearer than,
It seems to a faint and faltering man,
Often the struggler has given up,
When he might have captured the victor's cup,
And he learned too late when the night slipped down,
How close he was to the golden crown.

Success is failure turned inside out–
The silver tint of the clouds of doubt,
And you never can tell how close you are,
It may be near when it seems so far,
So stick to the fight when you're hardest hit–
It's when things seem worst that you must not quit.

- Anonymous

Now you have read through my chapter, my very first published writing, thank you very much. I have started my journey and I hope that you, too, will begin your journey and make it count. Do not quit till you complete what you planned out from the beginning. Enjoy every moment of it, create lots of memories, make friends along the way and you will have a great journey!

About James Lee

James Lee served as a Naval Officer in the Republic of Singapore Navy for 12 years before breaking out into the entrepreneurial world. He is a strong believer in innovative and creative methods of wealth creation and value adding to society through incubating ideas, assembling resources and making things happen. In the early years of his military career, James was awarded the Sword of Honour in 1995 (Top Cadet in Cohort) and later was among the few nominees for the Spirit of Enterprise Awards in 2008 (Singapore).

He is a firm believer in the strength of the team and enhancing productivity through effective teamwork. When he was first presented with a huge travel business opportunity in late 2010, there were practically no activities in Singapore. He saw that as a great opportunity for him to rise to the occasion and take on the leadership role in creating momentum in his part of the world. He has achieved the highest status in the company he represents and he is currently the top income earner in Asia within the company.

James enjoys giving back to society and has served in the community and grassroots organization for more than 10 years. Now, with this amazing business opportunity, he is able to travel the world with great people he will meet and to forge great friendships along the way. And he will be able to help thousands of people to realize their dreams and touch the lives of many with this amazing business.

Chapter 14

Ultimate Living
through Sacrificial Giving

BY LAUREN ESCOBAR-HASKINS

"I have found among its other benefits, giving liberates the soul of the giver."

- Maya Angelou

My simple, all-American upbringing held many blessings. I was part of a stable, church-going family. I spent summers outdoors with few cares, laughing and playing with neighborhood kids. I attended good schools, took exciting family vacations every year, and enjoyed skiing in the long Minnesota winters. My family loved me, and my future seemed bright. A rule-abiding people-pleaser, I was protected from the world's harsher realities.

Looking back, I see I that was in young suburban la-la land. I had done nothing to build my privileged life, yet I received all the benefits. I suffered no real hardships or trials and didn't even watch the news—it was too negative, and I didn't like the mood it put me in.

Who could blame me for enjoying my comfortable bubble? People who have it made don't usually go in search of difficulties or responsibility. However, without my even realizing it, some of my biggest blessings and attitudes were also some of my biggest handicaps because I had it so easy.

Thankfully, I began to notice a lack of influence, impact and meaning in my life. I do realize that the "All-American Dream" is what so many parents work tirelessly to provide their kids, and I don't mean to sound ungrateful for all the positive experiences in my life, but it was a good thing when, at 22, my life took a more "adventurous" turn.

A recent culinary school graduate, I'd just gotten started on my own, managing a nice restaurant and living in a cute apartment in a hip neighborhood. I was independent.

Before long, I fell in love with an outstanding, handsome man. Jay, a musician with two kids and a strong faith, is unlike anyone I'd ever met before. As a teacher of court-ordered parenting classes for men in our city, he had a passion for helping others. His character and attitude toward life were overwhelmingly attractive to me.

I'd never met anyone who cared as much about their convictions, or was as willing to stand up for their beliefs, as Jay. Where I came from, no one ever seemed to disturb the peace. Authentic feelings were often ignored, and we were always "happy." In fact, our whole world was "happy." But after I met Jay, the world seemed to have much more need of action, compassion and love.

However, my parents were not thrilled that I was dating him. Jay had kids, and it was also a challenge for my parents to identify with his background and positions on life. Their stance put a lot of strain on me, and I wasn't sure how to handle the tension when we were all together.

It's natural to want approval, so I found it hard to go against my parents' preconceived ideas of what type of man I should be with. Their approval, support and encouragement—as well as their feelings of pride in me—now all seemed uncomfortably in question.

I know my parents saw the challenges that taking on two kids would present. I'm sure they also looked at Jay's rough city background and compared that to my squeaky-clean life in the safe suburbs. My mother warned me in no uncertain terms that life with Jay would be challenging.

Others also voiced opinions. A close friend asked, "Why would you give up your freedom to be with someone who has kids?" To me the answer was clear: Jay was an authentic, good person, with more passion and character than anyone else I knew. Plus, we were deeply in love.

I realized that it was time for me to stand up for what I believed, and I believed in Jay and me together.

A month into our relationship, we got disappointing news. State funding was being cut, and Jay was laid off from the job he was passionate about. This was hard on him. He loved encouraging these men and watching them grow into their roles as fathers. Now jobless, Jay was forced to seek employment in a tough economic climate.

Another pressure came when Jay decided it was time for me to meet his kids and to let his ex-wife know about us. We were serious, and the kids would now be around me much more often. This freaked me out a little. I could see that Jay was a wonderful father, but I got nervous about how I would fit in and how serious we were getting. I liked kids, but being a stable figure in their lives was all new to me. As if adapting to these changes weren't enough, what happened next shocked us all.

One evening, Jay said he felt like a lightning bolt had stricken half his body. He was young, only in his early thirties, so it was hard to fathom the doctor's report that he'd suffered a heart attack. Our exciting "adventure" seemed to be getting scarier and more serious all the time.

I tried to process what was happening and to be strong and supportive. I helped with some of the logistics with the children as Jay regained his strength, but the weight of those days seemed unbearable, as both his career and now his health were in question.

Fortunately Jay's health eventually improved, and he even found a new job. We were ecstatic—this was the very hope we needed, and things were finally looking up.

One day Jay proposed. But despite the exciting prospects for our future, life continued to throw us some curveballs. For example, before the wedding I found out that I was pregnant. This upset my parents, and I felt like a disappointment to them. I withdrew from them and felt very isolated, ashamed and alone in what should have been a time of joy.

Around the same time, Jay was diagnosed with a stage II nodular melanoma, a serious form of skin cancer. Immediate surgery and follow-up radiation were now on Jay's plate, while nonstop morning sickness and wedding planning kept my head spinning.

To top it all off, when his ex-wife found out that we were getting married and having a baby, she seemed to make it her mission to prevent me from bonding with the kids. Jealous behavior and nasty schemes caught me completely off guard. As a happy and good girl, I'd never really had any conflict with anyone. But this woman was apparently *not* happy, and she seemed to thrive on conflict. My anxiety over this situation was exhausting.

I began to have doubts. What was happening with my life? Would Jay be okay? Did I deserve all this trouble and disapproval? Would I ever feel close to my family again? Would the children have a father to take care of them? I had no answers. I felt powerless, but it was a feeling I eventually learned to overcome.

Today, I'm happy to say that Jay and I are in a much better place. We have our three beautiful and healthy children, and Jay's health is stable. We've been blessed in our careers as well as financially. My relationship with my parents is much more relaxed, and I've even founded a cause that supports women in blended families. I have a passion for sharing the tangible tips and wisdom I've learned as a stepmother, and love encouraging other women in their journeys. I'm even writing a book about blended families.

So how did I get to this place of "ultimate living" despite all my trials? The keys are in sacrificial giving. The key concepts are:

Sacrificial For*giving*

Sacrificial Thanks*giving*

Sacrificial Resource Giving

Spin the Give Up Mentality

Be warned, however. These practical concepts aren't for those who want only a simple pick-me-up. No, they are for those who are *truly ready* to evolve their lives into something better.

Sacrificial *Forgiving*

Forgiveness can be humbling, but extremely liberating. For a long time, I thought I would forgive my family, friends and Jay's ex-wife only once they understood how their judgments and mistreatment hurt me. If I'd stuck with that plan, I could still be waiting to forgive, wasting a lot of time and good living.

Despite how we may want people to understand the hurt they've caused, waiting for them to apologize simply doesn't work. You cannot learn a lesson *for* someone. You can't demand apologies (or really even expect them) from anyone. Sure, acknowledgment from them would be wonderful, but you absolutely can choose to come to a place of forgiveness and wholeness that isn't contingent on anyone else's behavior. How freeing!

If I had waited for Jay's ex-wife to apologize, I'd probably still be waiting, stuck, and not moving forward. That thought wasn't attractive to me at all, so I sacrificed my pride. I chose to forgive so I could ultimately be free. Suddenly, my well-being and freedom were no longer contingent on her behavior.

Once I forgave, I found peace in my relationships. I had more self-control, I became a better listener, and I was more confident. I was even inspired to love my enemies, which resulted in more love coming my way. Forgiveness will result in doors opening in your life.

Sacrificial Thanks*giving*

During those hard early days with Jay, as I focused on what was going wrong, I became less grateful for what was going right. Having a thankful heart for the things you do have, rather than focusing on your lack, is a big game-changer spiritually. I didn't even notice that I wasn't being grateful, but then I wasn't really focusing on the positives.

I once heard Joyce Meyer say something profound. She said, "Complain and remain; praise and be raised." What a wakeup call! Immediately, I challenged myself to have an attitude of thanksgiving, and I started giving thanks for the little things, like a warm shower. Sometimes that felt like about all I had to be thankful for. With everything going on in my life, I was a little preoccupied with the negative side of things. But at least it was a start.

Once I made a habit of being thankful, suddenly I seemed to have more to be thankful *for*. As I practiced thankfulness, my outlook on life got better and I felt better. I couldn't believe the difference. Thanksgiving is the key to changing the glass from being half-empty to half-full.

Sacrificial Resource Giving

I used have a very poor attitude about giving. I always thought Jay and I would give once we got in a better financial situation, or once the wedding was over, or when things with Jay's health were better, or once the baby was born. I always had an excuse. It seemed impossible for us to give financially, so we rarely did.

Looking back, I don't really know what prompted us to start sacrificially giving. Possibly it was our internal moral meters simply knowing it was the right thing to do. Or maybe we gave because we knew firsthand what a blessing gifts could be.

Anyhow, we started giving $400 to a local cause every month. For some, $400 a month might be only a modest amount while, to others it may be half their income. For our family, it was a significant amount. And really that is my point: the amount should be significant.

Whether it's your time, money or energy, make sure that what you give is something you hold precious. This means that giving your old clothes to Goodwill may not be enough. Although that's an admirable way to clean out your closets, your old clothes are no longer precious to you. Therefore, you may need to evaluate ways you can sacrificially give more of the resources that are valuable to you.

Jay and I often noticed that after we gave, huge opportunities and blessings would come our way. I now challenge myself to look for ways to give sacrificially, and I always view it as an investment. Investments cost you something up front, but ultimately they provide returns.

Spin the Give Up Mentality

Finally, I'd like to suggest that you give up. Let go of anything that holds you back from ultimate living. For example, I couldn't continue to complain about my circumstances *and* hope to have an enjoyable day. I could either have an enjoyable day or complain, bringing my spirits down—but not both. So give up!

In your trials and tribulations, know that you are not alone. We all have them from time to time, some more than others. Some trials are unfair, some can last years, some just days, and some catch you totally off-guard. But remember that you're not powerless. You can be powerful in the midst of it all. You can have a great life even when hardship comes your way. The key is sacrificial giving. These keys work for everyone, and they can help you experience ultimate living yourself.

About Lauren Escobar-Haskins

Lauren Escobar-Haskins is a 25-year-old mother, entrepreneur, author and baking enthusiast. She has a passion for good food and great fun, balanced with a lifestyle of health and wellness. Lauren was raised in Eagan, Minnesota, a suburb of Minneapolis/St. Paul. Following high school, she attended the Florida Culinary Institute in West Palm Beach. Lauren currently resides in St. Paul in a beautifully blended family with her husband and three children. She is committed to helping others as they journey through the challenges, successes and diverse experiences of changing family dynamics—a journey she is all too familiar with. Her thoughts, inspirations and news about upcoming works can be found at www.laurenescobarhaskins.com.

Chapter 15

My Life Story:
Strong, Confident and Persistent

BY SHAN MCLENDON

"You never know what's around the corner. It could be everything. Or it could be nothing. You keep putting one foot in front of the other, and then one day you look back and you've climbed a mountain."

- Tom Hiddleston

I grew up in Fort Worth, Texas, in a moderate home where both my parents had to work to provide a decent life for my little sister and me. All through my childhood, I knew I was privileged to have both of my parents together in our home—most of my friends didn't have that. My mom and dad both had good jobs at the Postal Service, but they had to put in a lot of hours in order to provide the life we had.

Dad would drop us off at a babysitter's on his way in for the late shift, and then Mom would pick us up in the early morning hours when her shift was over. Their different shifts, and the number of hours they put in, meant that we weren't often home together at the same time. These were the sacrifices my parents made to provide the best for us.

As I got older, they put in even more time at work, but they were able to get better hours, so we got to see each other more as a family. Even though I had a good childhood, I knew at a young age I didn't want the same life when I grew up. I told myself that I'd be rich someday so I could be home with my family more.

I used to dream about hitting it big, like the people I saw on *The Lifestyles of the Rich and Famous*. I couldn't understand why my parents didn't fill out the Publishers Clearing House form so they, too, could win and stop working. After all, the TV commercials always showed how happy the people were when they won the sweepstakes. And then one day, it happened—I saw the thick Publishers Clearing House envelope in the stack of mail! I was so excited. I just knew it was our turn for the big time.

But alas, it was only an advertisement, not a letter telling us we'd won. Undaunted, I filled out the paperwork and affixed the stickers in the right places, over the little cars and houses on the form, so we could win and my parents could finally stop working. Needless to say, we never won, and I gave up hope on that dream.

For several years my father, whom I always saw as a fighter, a strong man and a great supporter, had an Amway business, which he believed would replace his income from work. Although he was never successful at it to that level, he did make some money. In fact, he tried a number of businesses while I was growing up but was never able to replace his full income. After several years, he gave up and just stayed focused on his work, putting in the hours necessary to increase our lifestyle. Mom was in school during my younger years and dedicated herself to her job and raising us kids. She, too, is very strong and believed in sacrifice. I knew I had a good, strong family and felt very blessed as a child.

I'm so grateful for the solid foundation my parents laid in our lives, because I needed it during my school years. I went to some very rough schools. The area I grew up in (Forest Hills) wasn't the worst 'hood around, but it was far from the best. I remember being in the sixth grade when the Crips and Bloods first really hit the scene in Texas, and crack rock was flooding the streets. Everyone wanted to be a gangster and gain street credibility. Even some of my friends that I used to play and ride bikes with decided to gang bang and sell dope. Everyone had a pager and a gun by the age of 15 to show they were hard.

Street credibility was everything in those days, as it still is today. I saw my first riot in the seventh grade in the school cafeteria at lunch. While part of me was afraid, the other part was excited by how dangerous it was, and by the fact that I was associated with such a hard school. I got into more fights in the seventh and eighth grades than I did in the rest of my school years combined.

But I had a secret: I wasn't the hard "gangster" type I pretended to be. Deep down, I just wanted to be a pretty-boy player who dressed nicely and tried to catch the pretty girls. Even so, all it took was for one person to think I was soft to start the domino effect. I never backed down from a confrontation. Once, I even got jumped in the hallway by four guys over a girl. I definitely didn't win that one, but I did gain respect for fighting back and not running.

Courage could either get you respect or get you killed in the 'hood. High school was a little better. I found my crowd. I played football, ran track and was in the marching band, which was considered cool at the all-black school I attended. The band, unlike the football team, taveled to games with the girls. In high school, that was cool. Everyone had a travel partner.

But the flip side of high school, at least the one I went to, was that now all the thugs had cars. Which meant they could do drive-bys and torment kids at rival schools in the area. I lost a few friends in high school to gang violence those four years. One of my best friends was killed due to gang violence just two weeks before graduation during our senior year. More people we grew up with died in those four years than have died in my adult life.

There is an old saying, "The 'hood will take you under." It will, if you don't have the support at home to keep you focused. Thank God for my strict parents and their rules that, at the time, seemed ridiculous. I credit those rules for saving me from an early death.

Once I graduated from high school, I went straight into junior college and completed four classes that summer. I'd been so conditioned by my parents that I would go to college that that's what I did. I decided to become an engineer—but only because that's what my father wanted me to do. I chose that major to make him proud of me, but honestly, I had no idea what I wanted to do with my life.

Adjusting to my first year of four-year college, away from home at Prairie View A&M University, was a struggle for me because I had never been on my own before. The fact that I was so independent was new to me, and it was hard to stay focused. I didn't have anyone telling me to get up and get ready for school or asking if I'd done all my homework. I was totally on my own without supervision. And like a lot of kids in this situation, I relaxed my standards. Instead of reading, writing and 'rithmetic, I focused on drinking, partying and smoking pot. I didn't totally lose focus on school, but I didn't truly apply myself as I knew I should have, especially considering I was going to school on my parents' hard-earned dime.

My Life Story: Strong, Confident and Persistent

I knew I needed to decide what I was going to do with the rest of my life, but I didn't know where to start. I'd never had my own bank account, had never written a check, had never really had to think past asking for permission for everything I did. As a child, my life had been structured; I'd been sheltered by my parents' strict rules. Even in high school, I hadn't been allowed to go out very much.

I was unprepared for the level of independence that being away from home afforded me—unprepared and ill-equipped to handle it. By the end of my freshman year at Prairie View, I did have enough sense to know that I needed to change my surroundings if I was going to complete college. I informed my parents that I hadn't failed anything but that I wasn't excelling either. I needed to change schools, and I needed to be closer to home, so I enrolled in the University of North Texas. This was a completely different college experience. I was able to get a job, and I opened my first bank account. It felt good to be working and not asking my parents for money all the time. I was excited about finally taking these first steps toward adulthood.

Unfortunately, I found myself racing toward adulthood too soon. On March 21 of that year, two weeks before my twentieth birthday, my girlfriend gave birth to our first son, Isaiah. I was nervous because I didn't know what I was going to do. I knew I had to be a good father and raise my son. I knew being a loser or an absent father wasn't an option for me because of how active my father had been in my life. I decided to get married and join the Army.

Because I had two years of college credits, I went in as a PF2. Shortly after I joined, my wife became pregnant again. My son was only five months old, and I already had another child on the way. My first thought was to get out of the Army, go back home and find a job, but my drill sergeant told me I should stay. He said the Army would get me ready for the real world. Plus, I would make more money with two kids, and it wouldn't be as hard to survive. Following his advice, I stayed in and was stationed in Fort Campbell, Kentucky, at the 101st Airborne division.

After two months in Kentucky, I went back to Texas and packed up my family. My son didn't really know me because I'd been in training and had missed most of his first year. My wife was in her third trimester and ready to give birth. At first everything was great, but slowly as time passed we started having problems. These problems weren't like the "girlfriend issues" that I'd had in the past. These were real-life issues that I'd thought I was ready for in a marriage. My wife had already lived on her own when I first started dating her, and she knew how to survive in the real world, but I was still learning. However things seemed better once my second son, Jordan, was born. I was just so proud because now I had two boys. What could make a man more proud than to have two beautiful, healthy boys?

In the Army, I went to Airborne School to jump out of helicopters. In Jump School, I felt like I was starting to achieve success, and in a way I was—not many people I knew would have jumped out of a helicopter while it was in the air. But after a little over two years in the Army, I was honorably medically discharged because I had developed arthritis in my spine and could no longer do any of the physical work I'd been doing as a mechanic without making it worse. Shortly after we moved back to Texas, my marriage finally cratered and we decided to divorce.

I knew that as a single dad of two boys, it would be hard to date. "How do I find success in life?" I asked myself. The answer was simple: *By not giving up.* I had a number of jobs during this time. I was able to rise to the level of supervisor or manager in each one. As I matured, I began to notice that people listened to me and believed in me. I had a job in the mortgage industry that I really liked, and I worked my way into management, but this time I made a good living, so I thought.

My new wife, Tamara, and I together brought in more than $120,000 a year—good money in Texas. We bought a 3500-square-foot home, had two nice cars, and my kids had everything they wanted. But still, I know there's more out there for us. I asked my wife why I can't seem to find the vehicle that will get us to success. She is a wise woman. She said, "If you look back on your life, you will see success."

"How come we aren't rich yet?" I asked.

"Look back at where you've been and how you've turned it all around," she said. "Your life is a great success to a lot of people. Some people would have given up a long time ago. Only the strong will survive, and you are strong, confident and persistent. Your vehicle is its way to success."

My wife was right. Success isn't a destination, it's a journey. In my journey, I'd found a few different vehicles that would lead me to financial success.

About Shan McLendon

Shan has had a few opportunities that have led him to success, but not to the level of success he has been striving for. With each business venture he found himself time broke. He has been focused on ways to achieve financial stability at a young age but has fallen short of the success level he desires. It is Shan's philosophy that if you fail at something, the worst thing you can do is to give up and lose focus of your goals. Instead, he believes that you make your dreams a reality by doing, not dreaming, and that determination and focus will equal success as long as you totally believe and continue to strive for it.

Chapter 16

Conquering the Cycle of Abuse
BY ESTHER FONTAINE

"When something hurts, it is a signal that something's wrong and must be changed."

- God

January 2012.

Burning tears flow uncontrollably; I can feel the sting on my cheeks and chin as they soak my shirt front. My head is pounding with dizziness from the alcohol, my heart empty, and my spirit full of enormous pain; and yet laughter rolls from the other room as company visits. The house is full of people, yet I sit alone feeling the absolute desperation of defeat and loneliness. The pain is so huge it's hard to breathe. I choke on my tears as the snot runs down my face. My body shakes with aggravation, and my cries are guttural, life-aching. I take a handful of pills and lie fetal, begging for God to deliver me. As I fade into sleep

I say to myself, "They were right. Everyone who said it to me all my life, they were right." Their words play again in my mind, "You'll never amount to anything. You never finish anything you start. Nothing is ever good enough for you. What makes you think you're so special? You always think you deserve more."

The words whirl around in my head. Images of my life begin to bombard me; the physical abuse, sexual abuse, screaming, leaving job after job, all the failed relationships, guilt over my kids, loss—over and over. Anger over the curse of my mental illness crashes in. I just want to die. I sink into a dark place, waiting for relief in the light of the tunnel to heaven. *I just want the pain to go away.*

Morning comes and I'm initially pissed off to be alive. I think, "Seriously, is this all there is to life?" I'm one huge failure. I've accomplished nothing that I've set out to do. I'm 48, with no retirement savings set aside and I'm dead-ass broke. My dreams for myself have all gone unfulfilled, as have my promises to my family. What's worse, I can foresee no hope for my future.

Then something strikes me.

I am alive.

I should be dead. Actually, I should have been dead a number of times for decisions I made in my life. But in that moment, as I poured my coffee, I had a surreal epiphany. I stopped—really stopped in that moment—and realized that God was not finished with me yet. I said, "God, please take my pain." But in my spirit I heard Him say, "NO." He said, "Esther, learn from your pain and use it to change your life. For when something hurts, it is a signal that something's wrong and must be changed."

Where did my pain come from? I know some of it stemmed from a lifetime of abuse. The life I lived created stress, which in turn triggered my innate bipolar disorder. On top of all that, I'm a lesbian. So not only did I have negative programming from my childhood to overcome, I had a lifelong condition of mental illness in addition to the social challenge of being a gay Christian. All of those issues played a role in my developing a stubborn mindset. But as for what lay at the root of my struggles and chronic failures in life, I knew there was more than just these issues. It was right in front of me, and it gave me bigger pain than all the others combined. It was *me*, the true inner me, that caused my failures.

I've spent my entire adult life using my past as an abused child, my mental illness and sexual orientation as crutches for my failures. I made them excuses, creating a mindset where I justified my behaviors and owned my limitations. These excuses allowed me to avoid placing the blame for the reality of my failures where it belonged: squarely on me, myself and I. I realized that I wanted to die because I hated myself and all that I had chosen to become. And it was a choice. As Johnny Wimbrey says, "No one loves Johnny like Johnny loves Johnny." Well, no one hated Esther like Esther hated Esther.

I had become everything I never wanted to become. I was negative, abusive, a fraud, a thief, a cheater, a liar and a bully. I had become a chronic failure, and I was filled with resentment, hatred and frustration because of those repeated failures. The failures in my life came into existence because I had been programmed to believe the biggest lie I was ever told. The lie is, "Sticks and stones will break your bones but names will never hurt you." Those words are a lie. I guarantee I can remember far more the hurtful words that were said to me than I can the actual hits and blows. The Bible says that words have power and life. They also have the power to kill. Words can kill the drive to succeed, to be more and do more. They can kill belief in oneself. They killed any belief I had that I deserved to fulfill my destiny. And they choked out any belief that I could achieve success. But worse and more powerful still than the start of that programming was the choice that I made as an adult to perpetuate it. I'm an intelligent, educated person and I would get so angry at myself because I kept doing the same things over and over, repeating the same destructive patterns of behavior. Just before success would manifest, I'd yet again sabotage myself and create failure instead. Why did this keep happening? Because I hated myself and didn't believe I deserved any level of success.

So why did I hate myself?

During a casual conversation with my friend Cindy one day, she said, "It's not who you are on the outside, it's who you are on the inside that counts." Well, we've all heard that a lot of times, but she meant it in a different way. She said, "It's not how you present yourself in public, but how you act behind the closed doors of your home. It's how you treat those closest to you that really matters in life, and we should never compromise on being the best we can with our family." That really struck me. In fact, it actually haunted me every day for two weeks, both while I was awake and in my dreams. From that point on, everything I did I began to run through that filter, and it only worsened my self-hatred.

I had people in my network of business partners who would edify me for being kind and loving. They would praise me for the helpful tasks I did and applaud my ability to teach and mentor others. But their praise began to burn me like coals upon my head. Their view of me no longer made me feel good about myself. Instead, now it made me feel angry because, unbeknownst to them, I was a fraud. My home life and my public life were out of balance; they didn't sync up, and I was a fraud. Writing this chapter in this book may result in a lessening of respect in that arena for me, but it doesn't matter because this is the time for me to change my entire life. In order to break through to the next level of living life instead of surviving life I have to be completely honest, and seek and create action toward my goals. So here comes the hard part, the part where I own up to my past so I can stop allowing it to define my future.

In public, I was kind and helpful. But at home, I was an abusive bully who dominated my family with angry words and actions. I busted property and threw rage-filled tantrums. Each one of my children has suffered the wrath of my physical abuse toward them. I've beaten them, most often in rages of anger. I abused their spirits by screaming negative words and curses at them. I lost my two oldest children because I put them in an environment where not only did I abuse them, but I allowed another person to abuse them as well. They have to live with nightmares in their lives because of the choices I made. I manipulated my kids and stepkids, pitting them against each other and causing dissent in our family. I lied my way through life, which destroyed my credibility with everyone I was ever close to. I've cheated on every relationship I've ever been in. I've hit my partner, and I've cursed horrifying words on her and her family. I would choose to buy alcohol over groceries so I could have my fun, regardless of what my family needed. I was a full-blown, out-of-control, abusive bully at home, terrorizing my children and my partner. Then I'd walk out the door and act as some big shot at work and in network marketing. I was nothing but a fraud and blamed everyone else for my failures. Well the words Cindy Medrano said to me that day haunted me because I knew what she said was the truth. I was living a double life, and my only excuse was me. My choices created my own defeat. Deep inside, I didn't want to be that person anymore. I knew God had something bigger for me. But there was only one way to get it—I had to change. So how did I stop the destructive patterns and turn it all around? How did I master my failures?

I made a decision and followed it with action. I had to develop a system of success in order to overcome myself. The system for me was this:

1. Admit what the problem was. It was me—not my past, not others; it was me.

2. I had to forgive myself and the past and not allow it to define me.

3. I had to change my mindset; find a way to change my thinking.

4. I had to find someone to be accountable to, whom I trusted and would listen to.

I admitted I was the problem. I asked God and several others to forgive me, and I worked to forgive myself. I chose to rewrite the ending of my life. Changing my thinking is a continuous, daily task. Sometimes it's a chore, but I do it because I do not want to be that person again. How do I change my thinking? Well, "garbage-in, garbage-out," as they say. I now choose things other than garbage to put in my mind. Every day, I purposely read materials that will enhance my spirit. I read the Bible and many books like this one you are reading today. I listen to music because it feeds my soul. I stop and think before I talk. I attend seminars that build my belief in myself, in my business and in others. I listen to a variety of audio CDs that promote positive thinking and personal growth. I teach what I learn so it can manifest in me more. I work with a couple of mentors with whom I am completely honest, even when it humiliates me to be. They hold me accountable to what I said I want to do and achieve. They care about me so they don't allow me to own my limitations. And they won't judge me, which could create a breakdown. Instead, they advise and critique me in order to create my breakthroughs.

I finally submitted to God and hold myself accountable to Him more than anyone else, because it is He who blesses us and truly loves us unconditionally. I had to realize that I had no authority to hate myself. God created me to be successful. He created me competent and capable to fulfill the life He envisioned for me. I had no right to hate his amazing creation. I list my submission to God last in this chapter, because that's what I did last, but submitting to God really must be the *first* thing we do in order to overcome failure and achieve any type or level of success.

I decided to expose myself in this book at the risk of losing a lot of respect and business contacts, but in doing so I gain far more. Perhaps this story will provide an opportunity for others who live life as an abuser to choose to be honest with themselves and change. Abuse is a generational curse, and many of us say, "I don't want to do that to my kids," but then we abuse them anyway. We use excuses like, "That's the way I was brought up." But that doesn't make it right. It's your choice to stop. It takes action to get help. It is possible to break the curse and create a new legacy for your family and yourself. Change is a choice, and the only way to become a new person is to become a new person. Life doesn't generally change miraculously overnight. As a matter of fact, for most of us, it's a daily journey filled with obstacles to overcome. For awhile, it actually may become a little more difficult, because now we're on a mission to repair and grow. Anyone who chooses to participate in their own rescue can be rescued, but remember that it's a choice followed by purposeful actions.

I challenge and encourage those who are abusers to stand up and get help. Fulfill your destiny of love and life that God created us all to have. I will never believe the lie that, once an abuser, always an abuser. *Anyone* can change. It is a choice—a process of actions—sometimes uncomfortable and frustrating, but in the end rewarding and fulfilling. It's time to live life instead of survive it. God's peace.

About Esther Fontaine

Esther A. Fontaine was born in Butte, Montana, in 1964. She spent her formative years in Portland, Oregon, between 1972 and 1979. She then returned to Montana and graduated from Napa Police Academy in 1986 and the University of Great Falls with degrees in Sociology and Criminal Justice.

Esther worked as a correctional officer at Montana State Prison and then spent 25 years in transportation. She is currently a motivational speaker, leader and mentor as well as a successful network marketer. A lesbian with three children, two step-children and three beautiful grandchildren, Esther is a successful life-changer.

Contact Information:
estherfontaine@gmail.com
www.estherfontaine.worldventures.biz

Chapter 17

Stepping Out On Faith
BY MICHAEL PARKER

"Faith isn't the ability to believe long and far into the misty future. It's simply taking God at His Word and taking the next step."
- Joni Erickson Tada

To "step out" is to take action, and to have faith is to believe in something greater than yourself or your circumstances, whether you can see it or not. I have faith in God, and I'd like to share my story to show you how important it is to stay in alignment with and focused on Him.

I come from a neighborhood that wasn't the best. We didn't have much, but as long as I had my mom and grandparents, I was okay. They wanted better for me than what they had, and they did whatever it took to keep me grounded and away from negative influences. They were my rocks, and my young mother raised me to be a respectful, responsible, God-fearing young man with a strong mind, dependant on no one else. I wasn't just told this—I saw the example she lived out daily. My mom also taught me to be kind-hearted and caring, because you never know what someone might be going through.

I later fell in love with a beautiful girl who'd been taught the same values. We had an instant connection and couldn't imagine life without each other, so we got married and began our journey.

A few years ago, she and I were off to a good start. We'd just built a house, had a new car and a baby on the way. We had a great relationship, and it seemed that things just kept getting better. It was obvious to us that God brought us together for a reason. He gave us a purpose, but He also wanted to ensure that we'd stay strong in Him throughout everything. We didn't know it then, but we were about to be tested.

My wife and I worked for a small HVAC company. I was the shop foreman, and she handled the payroll in the office. My main function was to ensure that all the materials for each job we contracted were complete in time. We had jobs in and out of town, and when the field guys came in we wasted no time, quickly loading their trailers for the new job. Our company was built on the pride of customer satisfaction; we had deadlines to meet and promises to keep. It was a good system; we did very well, and our client base was growing. In fact, we had to add manpower to keep up both in the shop and in the field. As the volume increased, the owner hired a family member as my new supervisor. He seemed cocky, and I had my doubts about him, but I kept things moving. I told myself to be accepting and to "just be the best me that I can be." This attitude helped me handle things I had no control over and gave me a sense of maturity in an uncertain situation.

In our small company, everyone knew about whatever was happening in the office. My new supervisor's office was in there, and soon it became apparent that he was having some issues at home. Every day was a bad day for him, and it was rough on my wife and me as we had to deal with his moods.

One day it must have gotten pretty bad for him. He came out to the shop to de-stress from his issues and to show me a different welding method. As he was demonstrating it, he accidentally backed into some metal, sticking himself in the back. Now all of his frustration, stress and anger came barreling directly at me, like it was my fault he'd hurt himself. He was yelling at me for something he'd done.

During his tirade, I remained calm, only watching him get angrier. He finally shouted at me to "GET OUT!"

I took off my welding gear, shaking my head and smiling. I walked into the office, got my wife, and we left right then and there. We were stepping out on faith!

Some may not think it smart to walk out on a stable job, with a very pregnant wife now also out of work, especially with house and car loans. But *we* aren't just anyone—we are God's children! I wasn't going to stand there and let that devil destroy me. And I surely wasn't going to leave my wife there. We left, without turning back.

Now my wife had no idea what was going on, but she was right beside me the whole way out. Only when we were on our way home did she ask what had happened. She knew me well enough to not ask the right question at the wrong time. There's a time and place to discuss private matters, and in the office on the way out was not the place.

As I explained the situation, she understood. She and I usually were on the same page about things. But she did wonder why I was smiling as we left. I told her, "Because I know we'll be okay." And she was okay with that because she believed whole-heartedly not only in me, but also in us.

Stepping out on faith is wonderful, but you can't stop there. *You have to keep believing in yourself and trusting in God to guide you along your path to greatness.* If you let a little doubt or fear creep in, then your faith has grown smaller. Don't sit idly by "waiting on God," because He won't wait on you to eventually do what He's already asked of you. For your purpose to be accomplished, you need to take action and keep focused on Him. He's always there, He always listens and cares, but remember: Our God is a big God, and if you won't do His will, He'll spend His time elsewhere. He'll pay more attention to His children who *are* walking in His footsteps than those who choose to do it alone.

Now God will never leave nor forsake us; His word says so and it's true. But we often tend to leave *Him*. Your faith must stay steady. Do you recall the story of Jesus walking over to his disciples on the water (Matthew 14:22-33)? One of them, Peter, decided to step out onto the water and walk on it to where Jesus was standing. Stepping out there was alright; taking a few steps wasn't bad either, but when the winds picked up and the waves got bigger, Peter's focus shifted to those obstacles instead of staying on Jesus. Peter had stepped out on faith, but his actions didn't stay the course. As he began to sink, Jesus stretched out His hand to save Peter, saying, "You of little faith."

Have a faith that is steady. If you feel like you're sinking, just hold on. Stay strong and trust that everything will be alright. Know that, if needed, our Savior will save you as He saved Peter.

I know this first-hand, because I lost my focus in the midst of my storm…

By now we'd been out of work for a while, but we'd made arrangements with the bank regarding our home and car loans. A little time passed and we had our son, healthy as could be, and now our family was all together. But we learned quickly that having a child brings some disagreements in a household. Suddenly, things got strange. I had my way of how things should be done, and she had hers. Although we didn't argue (we never believed in that and still don't), we weren't on the same page anymore. We couldn't figure out what the problem was. This new frustration only added to the stress I felt looking for work.

During this time, the bank reneged on the deal we'd made. We'd agreed that my wife and I would pay what we could on our home loan and that the rest would be added to the end of the note. Suddenly, the monthly amount we'd agreed to wasn't acceptable. They wanted more, and they wanted it now. This meant my wife couldn't stay home with the baby, so we both found good jobs. This made things calmer for a while, but then we received a letter from the bank stating that someone new had taken our case, and they took the house too.

I wondered what else could go wrong, and I soon found out when our vehicle was repossessed. Nothing was going right, and I felt as if I was failing my family. There was nothing we could do, no one would work with us or even help us understand what was going on or why.

Since my wife and I didn't argue when things got bad, we did the worst thing you can do—not talk to each other at all, which put even more strain on us. Not being on the same page with or even speaking to the person you love is a horrible feeling. It changes things and separates you. The devil wants this separation, and God allowed it to happen in order to test us.

Now, every day was a bad one. We had to move, get a new vehicle, change our lifestyle and adjust to having a newborn. As bad as things were, they were about to get worse. If the Lord is going to get your attention for you to do His work, He will get it however He sees fit. Even though God was talking to us throughout our struggles, we were so caught up in them that *they* became our focus instead of Him. We now know that He was telling us to stop trying to do everything on our own, without Him. We heard only what we wanted to and paid attention to the wrong things—a mistake we learned the hard way. It took what happened next to finally get through to us.

My wife's grandfather was a quiet man. He and his wife had three sons, and as the first girl in their family, my wife was very close to him—and he was very protective of her. When I started coming around, he didn't say much, but he knew she was happy. When it came to marriage, however, we heard from him—he let us know he thought we were too young.

Eventually, Grampa and I found out that we were a lot alike. He saw that I was genuine and sensed that I could take care of his little girl, and I began to breathe a little easier knowing that he was alright with me.

So there we were, going through this storm on our own and not seeking God's guidance. One day my wife's grandmother called saying that Grampa wasn't doing so well; he was having a hard time breathing and wasn't responsive. Paramedics took him to the nearest hospital, and by the time we got there, he'd been hooked up to machines and wasn't awake. The doctors worked on him a long time, and we even tried talking to him to get him to wake up, but all to no avail. After several days, my wife had the strength and courage to uphold her Grandpa's wishes. He'd never wanted to be kept alive by machines, so she instructed the hospital staff to take him off of them. We were hopeful at first as his vital signs got better, but then they slowly began to weaken. There was nothing more anyone could do, so we waited.

It's devastating losing someone you love, especially when you respect them so much. While he lingered, I told him that everything would be okay, to rest and not fight anymore, not to worry about anything and that I'd take care of her. When he passed, the world stood still for a moment. For a while I wasn't sure we'd recover, but we eventually came to realize what we already knew—what doesn't kill us only makes us stronger.

I'm not saying that God brought Grampa home only as a wake-up call to us, but He did use it that way. It brought us closer, and our faith and marriage are now stronger than ever. We are building a successful business and don't have to worry about a mortgage or a car note. With God, all things work out. On a sad note, we later found out that the company we'd worked for closed down. The supervisor's mess brought the entire company down. Everyone there started to have issues at work and at home, and the place fell apart.

When issues or obstacles arise for us now, my wife and I have learned to look to God first. We have learned a lot of things, and now we're on an unlimited path to greatness. We're all here for a reason, which is to do God's work with His guidance and in His will. I urge you: *Don't let things go too far before you realize that you should be doing better with the life that God blessed you with.* You can have a beautiful life if you choose to use the sound mind that He gave you. Have faith, but also take action as a child of God and do His work.

About Michael Parker

Michael Parker is a God-fearing young family man, entrepreneur, author and soon to be a speaker. He comes from a lower-class suburb of the Dallas–Ft. Worth area of Texas. His surroundings didn't project a prosperous future, but his loved ones wouldn't let that hold him back. With the help, love and guidance of his mother and grandparents, he was set upon a path to do better in life than they had been afforded. Michael strives to help others see that, if they will believe, they too can achieve greatness in life, no matter how they started out. For the opportunity to speak with and/or do business with Michael, contact him at www.parker.unlimited@yahoo.com.

Chapter 18

A Recipe for Happiness...

BY DIANE POPOWICH

"If you can DREAM it, you can DO it."

- Walt Disney

I've always known that I have something special inside of me. I feel a little like a cross between Oprah and Tony Robbins, with a bit of the girl next door of Valerie Bertinelli mixed in. I know that I was put on this earth to inspire and empower people.

So what was holding me back? Why couldn't I "just do it" like Nike says? It's that easy, isn't it? But wait. What if I fail? What would people think of me? What would my dad think, what would my daughter think? What kind of role model would I be if I failed? What if, what if, *what if?* This is the mind game I played with myself for a long time. Sometimes I still do. Until I remember that it is up to *me* to participate in my own dreams. Then I ask myself, "What kind of role model would I be to my daughter if I *didn't* try?" Finally, I "got it" that it was time for me to live the life I dreamed of. After all, I have the dream; in fact, I've dreamed the whole movie! (And honestly? I wouldn't be surprised that someday it *will* be a movie.) But getting to that realization didn't just happen overnight.

When I was a child, I believed I could do anything—whether it was being a Mother Teresa, an Olympic figure skater or a mentor to millions. And I still firmly believe that the mindset "anything is possible" should be taught to every child. If children don't learn this in their early years, they'll grow up to have limiting beliefs as adults. As I grew older, I learned the feeling of embarrassment due to failure, even over something as insignificant as giving the wrong answer in front of classmates. But from the example of my friend, Terry Hitchcock, who ran 75 marathons in 75 days to prove that "nothing is impossible," I learned a valuable lesson: *Failure will negatively shape your life if you let it.* You must keep the mindset that failures are stepping stones to successes and remember that Anything is Possible!

Failure sure shaped mine. I had been a strong, athletic and confident figure skater. At least, that's how others defined me. I was Diane Popowich the accomplished figure skater, the one who woke up at 4:30 every morning to go to the rink and practice. But when I was 15, I started having excruciating pain in my feet. The doctor diagnosed me with rheumatoid arthritis and told me that I could never skate again.

As scary as that news was, I couldn't imagine a life that didn't include skating. Being very disciplined and dedicated, I didn't even consider quitting. I just *knew* that I could beat the odds, and decided to keep on skating. Shortly after, the U.S. Olympic Committee came to my town to audition teams to perform in the Opening Ceremonies of the 1980

Winter Games. My skating team auditioned, and we were chosen to be part of the Minnesota Olympic Precision team. I skated in those opening ceremonies. I was strong. I had no fear.

Even though I didn't know what I really wanted in life, I had always seemed to accomplish what I set out to achieve. On the surface, my early adulthood appeared to be no different. I got into a good college (TCU); I landed the first job I interviewed for, with Xerox (they actually recruited and hired me prior to graduation), and I even won some awards as top salesperson. I had a perfect life. Then I got married, and things started to change.

Looking back, I see that I probably married the wrong person for the wrong reasons. By the time I walked down the aisle, I was already "disengaged." Shortly after my wedding, I started to gain weight, my arthritis got worse, and before long I was walking with a cane. But at the time, I didn't really understand what was happening.

By the ten-year mark in our marriage, we lived in a premier neighborhood, and our daughter was just starting the first grade in a private school. But I was still miserable. At first, I didn't tell anyone about my marital issues, but I eventually confided in a few friends, one of whom was a neighbor. Then it happened—I discovered my husband was having an affair. To make matters worse, it was with the neighbor whom I'd confided in *and* I'd discovered it by walking in on them—ouch!

Insert emotional rollercoaster here. I needed to find out if I still had any "mojo" so I called all my old boyfriends—except the high school one—why couldn't I call David, I wondered. Then I realized it was because I still had some feelings for him. Yikes! Why hadn't I dealt with those feelings before? And the answer began to dawn on me. David had proclaimed his love for me just after college, and despite the fact that I loved him too, I'd pushed him away. But why did I do that? Why push him away if I loved him?

The more I thought about it, the more it started to make sense. It all went back to a horrible experience during my college years that I had buried deep down inside. David and I had decided to date other people while we were away at college so I started to date Gary and fell in love with him. Our relationship progressed and we slept together. I was sexually uneducated and I got pregnant. I couldn't possibly tell my parents; it would have ruined their plans for my future. So in my middle trimester, I decided to have an abortion. The experience still haunts me, and I as write about it, I relive the nightmare and tears are streaming down my face. I was all by myself, it was very painful and I remember vomiting profusely. I was wracked with guilt. How could I have been so stupid? The baby inside of me was five months old! I remember the feel and awful sound of a vacuum-like instrument inside of me, sucking the life out of me literally and figuratively.

This was the reason I had pushed David away from me. I'd pushed him away because I didn't feel worthy of him or his love. And so I distanced myself from him. I thought I was damaged goods. *I* decided he could never love me, and that I should stop the relationship before it got started again. So I did.

But the pain and deceit went deeper still. I was very close to my parents, and I felt that if they found out they wouldn't love me anymore. So I distanced myself from them, too, especially my father. My mom had unconditional love for her children, but I was very fearful of disappointing my dad. I had begun to realize I had been afraid of him my whole life. He demanded perfection, or at least that is what I felt. I felt his love was conditional. My whole childhood I had watched how hard he was on people who made mistakes. God knows, I wasn't going to make one! I'd grown up feeling that failures or mistakes were not options, and now I had failed, big time. I wasn't "perfect" anymore. I really wasn't worthy of *anyone's* love.

It began to dawn on me that I had married my husband, Tom, mainly because he had been accepting of my imperfections, which wasn't fair to either of us. Fortunately we did do something right, we had a beautiful daughter; she is truly the best part of my life. One thing I have realized is that I had been putting her under the same kind of pressure—setting her up to be perfect. She didn't want to fail at anything because she knew it would disappoint me. How ironic was that? Perfection does not exist. We all want the best for our children, but not allowing for mistakes or failure can cripple them from reaching higher in their lives.

Even though I'd had a strong foundation since childhood of believing that anything was possible, and despite the fact that I was able to achieve some great things, I still had the underlying limiting belief that I was not worthy. This led to some interesting highs and lows during the time my marriage was disintegrating.

For example, during this time I discovered a passion for cooking, and I loved having people enjoy my creations. I became a chef, started a catering company and got rave reviews for my famous spaghetti and turkey rosemary meatballs. I got requests to teach people how to make them, and I discovered that was a great way to really to connect with people. I began hosting team-building events, and *I AM* Magazine wrote an article about my "Power of Passion." Awesome as all that was, it wasn't paying all of the bills.

We couldn't keep the lights/gas on, literally. We couldn't pay for both the gas and electricity, so the gas was cut off. I remember heating water on the stove so I could warm my daughter's bath. We were even on food stamps! I went back to selling real estate. Our house went back to the bank, we lost both cars, and worst of all, I lost my dignity and self respect.

Why did I settle for this lifestyle? But at the same time, I sold 37 lofts in one day. I had buyers camping overnight to make purchases, and I found myself on the front page of the local newspaper's business section. Lows and highs; doubt and belief—it all seemed so crazy!

I moved in with my parents and started to rebuild. After my divorce was final, I sold a few successful developments and reestablished a resale business as well. Things started to look up, and I was eventually able to buy a home again. Then I got a letter from the IRS stating that, if I didn't pay them $138,000, they were going to take my home. The IRS apparently doesn't care what a divorce degree says about who owes what. I did it…I worked my tail off and was able to save our home, but it came at a cost.

I was so busy running our lives, paying all the bills and providing a stable environment for my daughter that I had to cancel a trip to Florida to visit my parents. A month later I got a call that my mom had had a massive stroke. Sadly, she passed away. *What* was so important that I had to cancel my trip to see my family? I started questioning the path I was on. That's when a friend shared another way for me to make a living that was more more fulfilling and that would allow me to gain some of my life back.

With that business came the world of personal growth and leadership development….Wow! I had been searching for this my whole life, and didn't even know it. It felt like I'd found my home. I cannot talk about it enough, read about it enough, listen to it enough or teach it enough. It was during this journey that I knew I'd found my purpose in life—to inspire and empower others. I connected with some amazing people who had broken through their own fears and limiting beliefs. I also learned about myself and how my experiences have shaped me and how other people's experiences shape them.

I've now started living "the bucket life," which is "living the life you dream about." For example, I had a life-changing experience where I helped build "bottle schools" in Guatemala using plastic bottles and other trash. While I was there, I shared with a mentor of mine that I really shouldn't have taken the trip because of some things going on in my life. (The "old me" would not have taken the trip.) He said, "This is *exactly* where you should be." And he was right.

On this journey, I learned about what's important in life. The people of Guatemala don't have much, but they are happy! They don't strive to "keep up with the Joneses" or care about job titles. And I bonded with the others on the trip; we are like family now. Because of this experience, I decided I was going to host spaghetti-and-meatball dinner events to raise money to build another school there, in honor of my mom. (And if *you* would like to learn more, please visit www.joaniesgift.com.)

My journey has also helped me to forgive my ex-husband and the neighbor for what they did. I have forgiven myself for my part in the breakdown of the marriage as well as my abortion. I was able to forgive my dad for not always loving me in the way I needed him to and to understand that he is a product of his own experiences. And my journey has also resulted in the development of VisionBodies, which is a tool to help people push through fear and live the life they dream about.

I've held onto and believed in my dreams, and now I am living them! I also believe that I will find the right relationship (now taking applications) for me; I know I am worthy. I will empower and inspire millions to know that "Anything is Possible." My worthiness and happiness comes from within me, not anyone else, and so does yours! I would like to share my recipe for happiness with you...the secret is in the sauce!

Recipe for Happiness

1. What is your dream? What are you making?

2. Have a plan and follow the recipe. Follow someone's recipe who has what you want.

3. Sautee confidence, strength and belief until their flavors blend together.

4. Add tons of passion!!!

   Figure out "why" you are making it. What makes your heart flutter? What could you do for hours, days and weeks, without interruption? What is driving you? Put that passion in a large pot and bring it to a boil.

5. Mix in tons of positive people who will support you and Stir vigorously! Their flavor will marinate with the confidence, strength, belief and passion.

6. Stir in chunks of hard work, remembering to work smart. Don't let anyone steal your dreams.

7. Spice it up by adding a mentor or two. This will add accountability and wisdom to your sauce.

8. Let it simmer with forgiveness and worthiness.

9. Sprinkle it with a WHOLE LOTTA LOVE!

10. Serve it piping hot over the foundation of "Anything is Possible."

Serves every soul on the planet!

Enjoy! Diane Marie

About Diane Popowich

Diane's daughter, Steph, is the reason Diane pursued the path to inspire and empower people to believe that anything is possible...to live the life you dream about. Diane is a figure skater and performed in the Opening Ceremonies of the 1980 Winter Olympics. An accomplished author, speaker and chef, Diane is highly sought after for her unique culinary engagements. She is involved in many projects, including building schools in Guatemala, DreamMissions, VisionBodies, LifeTools for Teens, and the Terry Hitchcock "Nothing Is Impossible Tour." In addition, she serves on the board of Single Parent Advocate. Diane is also the founder of www.TheBucketLife.com.

Chapter 19

Defining Moments

JIM ROHN

An Interview with Jim Rohn by Mike Litman (*Reprinted with the permission of Mr. Rohn*).

Litman

Over the last 38 years, spanning almost four decades, this individual has influenced people that have trained a whole class of personal development students. People like Mark Victor Hansen, Anthony Robbins, and more.

He's the author of dozens of books and cassettes, courses on success, on living a life that is your potential, and realizing your dreams.

Tonight, I will bring to you, the one, the only, Jim Rohn. Author of many books I've talked about. Tonight we're going to go A to Z on how you can live a life of success in business and in family.

How do you do that?

Why is he the mentor for millions of people worldwide?

Jim Rohn, my dime, your dance floor. Welcome to The Mike Litman Show.

Rohn
Hey, thanks Mike. I'm happy to be here.

Litman
Great. I know myself and everyone is very excited for you to share some wisdom tonight and talk about the concept of success and about the principles for achieving it in our next 57 minutes together.

I'd like to start out by defining the word. What does 'success' mean to Jim Rohn?

Rohn
Well, I think the ultimate success, which I teach in my seminar, is living a good life.

Part of it is income. Part of it's financial independence Part of it is objectives that you achieve, dreams coming true, family, children, grandchildren, good friends, productivity. It's a wide range.

It's all encompassing, the word "success."

It's not just your job, your income, your fortune. Not just your paycheck or your bank account. But everything. From all of your achievements during your life to trying your best to design a way to make it all give you a good life.

Litman
So, we're talking about design.

We'll get to ambition.

We're talking about goals. We're talking about planning. You talk about something in your literature.

You mention that success doesn't need to be pursued. It needs to be attracted.

What do you mean by that?

Rohn

That's true.

I was taught, starting at age 25 when I met a mentor of mine by the name of Mr. Shoaff. He taught me that success is something you attract by the person you become. You've got to develop the skills.

He talked about personal development: become a good communicator, learn to use your own language.

He talked about the management of time.

But primarily developing yourself, your attitude, your personality, developing your own character, your reputation. Then developing the skills. From sales skills to recruiting skills, to management skills, leadership skills, how to work with a variety of people. You know, the full list.

He taught me to work on myself, because I used to work on my job.

He said, "If you work on yourself, you can make a fortune." That turned out to be true for me.

He turned it all around and said, "Success is not something you run after, like a better job."

Although that is to be desired.

You've just got to ask yourself, "Am I qualified for doubling, tripling, multiplying my income by three, four, five?"

If I look at myself and say, "No, not really." Then I need to ask myself, "Who could I find? Where can I go that could pay me three, four, five times as much money?"

Then, you have to say, "At the present there probably isn't anyone. I can't just fall into a lucky deal."

But, if I went to work on myself immediately. Work on my attitude, personality, language, and skills. Then that begins the process of attracting the good job, the good people, and building a business or creating a career that could turn out to make you financially independent, perhaps wealthy.

Litman

Jim, so really what we are talking about is a change of mindset. Of changing our thinking and getting in tune with the universe.

Talk about something that you mentioned. Changing your language. Describe what that means.

Rohn

There is the language that can fit.

You can use careless language around home and around the community.

But, if you want to start stepping up, then you've got to learn the language. The corporate language. You've got to learn the sales language.

Then you've got to be careful not to be careless with your language in the marketplace. It can cost you too much.

You know, a guy that is inclined to tell dirty stories, inclined to use a bit too much profanity. It might be okay in the inner circle and at the bar or whatever. But when you start to move into the world of business and finance where you want to be successful, earn a better paycheck, move up the scale, you just have to be careful. So, one of the major things is your language.

Not just that, but learning the language of success. Learning how to treat people with respect. Giving people inspiration when they need it, correction when they need it.

The same thing as learning to work with your children.

Language opens the door for fortune. It opens the door for help. It opens the door for better living. It opens the door for a good marriage. It opens the door for a stable friendship.

A big part of it starts with our thinking, our attitude, and then a major part of it is the language we use.

Litman

Okay, something that we are sharing tonight with people worldwide now, is we are talking about an inner change, then the outer result.

So many times people are trying to change the outer, without changing the inner. Is that what we are talking about?

Rohn

Yeah, that's true.

The big part of it, of course, is to start with philosophy.

Making mistakes and judgments can just cost you so much in the marketplace, at home, with your family, whatever it is. Errors in judgment can really do us in. It can leave us with less of a life than we could've had.

We've got to learn to correct those errors whether they are errors in philosophy or something else.

My mentor asked once why I wasn't doing well.

I showed him my paycheck and I said, "This is all the company pays." He said, "Well, that's really not true. With that philosophy, you'll never grow."

I said, "No, no, this is my paycheck. This is all the company pays." So, he said, "No, no, Mr. Rohn. This is all that the company pays you."

I thought, "Wow, I'd never thought about that."

He said, "Doesn't the company pay some people two, three, four, five times this amount?" I said, "Well yes." He said, "Then this is not all that the company pays. This is all that the company pays you."

For your income to multiple by three, four, five, you can't say to the company, "I need more money." You've just got to say to yourself, "I need a correction in my philosophy. I can't blame circumstance. I can't blame taxes. I can't say it's too far, too hot, too cold. I've got to come to grips with myself."

That is really where it all begins.

It's corrections of errors in judgment and in your own philosophy.

Litman

We're talking about philosophy. Is it really like ironing down a purpose?

You're talking about the word "philosophy" to someone listening right now and they're trying to put it into actual practice.

Someone right now that's in a rut, lost, how do you go about the process of putting together a philosophy that excites you and that benefits others?

Rohn

You start with the easy stuff.

Ask most people, "What is your current philosophy for financial independence that you're now working on?" and usually the person says, "Gosh, I never thought about that."

Unless you have an excellent financial philosophy that gives you guidance to correct errors, accept some new disciplines, and make some changes, you can forget being financially independent.

Ask yourself, "What is your philosophy on good health?" Is it to cross your fingers and sort of let it go and if something goes wrong then you fix it?

The answer is no. You should try to learn up front.

Ask yourself, "What is your cholesterol count?" The average guy's philosophy is, "I don't know and I don't care. If something goes wrong, I will try to fix it."

But, by then usually it's too late. Now it'll cost you a fortune. It costs you time. Maybe even it costs you your life.

If someone can help you with errors in judgment, or help you correct your financial philosophy, your spiritual philosophy, your philosophy on a good relationship, that's where it all begins.

We go the direction we face, and we face the direction we think.

It's the things we think about and ponder. What are your values? What's good? What's not so good? What's the better way? What's the best way?

Unless we do some constructive thinking on that, we usually take the easier way.

Easy causes drift, and drift causes us to arrive at a poor destination a year or five years from now.

Litman

So, we're talking about increasing our self-awareness. We're talking about philosophy.

I want to transition to a concept of planning, but before I do, Jim, let's talk about something you have been talking about for decades.

You give people options and you give people a choice.

You say, "You can either be in somebody else's plan or playing in your own life." Can you talk about that?

Rohn

That's true. Some people sort of resign to letting somebody else create the productivity, create the business, create the job, and it seems to be easier for them to punch the clock and let everyone else have the responsibility. Then they go home and try to make the best of it.

But, I think it is also good to start pondering and thinking, "How could I take charge of my own life? Or whether I qualify for a better position where I am. Or whether I might create my own business, start something, developing from my personal productivity."

If we just sit back and not take responsibility, that is what happens. Then we fit into someone else's plans, rather than designing plans of our own.

If you don't have plans of your own to fill that vacuum, you're probably going to fit into someone else's plan.

Litman

Jim, what if you don't know what the plan is?

What happens to someone when they're at a job right now, 9 to 5, working the clock, they don't know what they're passionate about, they don't know where to go, where do they start?

Rohn

You don't have to operate from passion to begin with. You operate from necessity. My friend, Bill Bailey, said when he got out of high school he went to Chicago from Kentucky and the first job he could find was night janitor.

Someone asked him, "How come you settled for a job as night janitor?" He said, "Malnutrition."

So, the first passion is to survive. To somehow make it.

Then start to build from there with something that you could find to do even if it is distasteful.

You don't have to love what you do. Just love the chance or the opportunity to begin the process. Because where you begin is not where you have to end a year from now, five years from now, ten years from now.

You just begin, first of all, to correct errors.

Find something, anything, it doesn't matter what.

America is such an incredible country. Especially because the ladder of success is available for everybody.

If you have to start at the bottom and make your way to the top, who cares? As long as they let you on the ladder.

Then, if you study, and grow, and learn, and take classes, and read books, burn a little midnight oil, start investing some of your own ambition, I'm telling you, the changes can be absolutely dramatic.

That is what happened for me starting age 25.

Litman

At age 25, in a six-year period, you went from being broke to becoming a millionaire.

Obviously, you put this stuff into practice. You started your own, I'll use the words, "mental make over," changing your thoughts, changing your attitude.

It seems to me, and this is personal for me, Jim, this quote of yours influences me tremendously even today, "discipline versus regret."

Talk about the importance of that. Talk about how to live a disciplined life and stay disciplined so you can get what you want.

Rohn

It is true. We suffer one of two things. Either the pain of discipline or the pain of regret. You've got to choose discipline, versus regret, because discipline weighs ounces and regret weighs tons.

Litman

Say that again.

Rohn

Discipline weighs ounces and regret weighs tons.

The reason is because the regret is an accumulated effect a year from now, two years from now. When you didn't do the easy discipline.

It's like having a cavity in your tooth. The dentist says, "If we fix it now it's only $300, and if you let it go someday it's going to be $3,000."

So, the easier pain of the $300 and sitting in the chair for just a little while takes care of it.

But, if you let it go that's no good.

You know, the dentist says, "This cavity is not going to get better by itself. This is something you have got to take care of. You can't cross your fingers and hope it's going to go away. That's not going to help."

Whatever you see that needs to be corrected, you start taking care of it.

If you don't have a splendid diet, you've got to be incredibly thoughtful about how to change that.

If your kids don't have a splendid diet, you've got to say, "Hey, maybe I should give some attention to my kids and their diet."

Nutrition affects behavior I was taught at age 25. Nutrition affects learning. Nutrition affects performance. Nutrition affects vitality. Nutrition affects decision-making. Nutrition affects longevity.

My mother studied and practiced good nutrition and talked to me about it, an only child, and my father too, who lived to be 93.

The doctor told me that my mother extended her life at least 20 years by paying attention to nutrition and practicing the art.

The benefits are so incredible by taking a look at a few simple disciplines.

You know, if mom said, 'An apple a day," and the guy says, "Well, no. I'm not into the apple a day, I've got my fingers crossed and I think everything is going to be okay," you've just got to say, "This is a foolish person.'

It doesn't matter what it is. You don't have to take giant steps at first.

To have an incredible increase in self-esteem, all you have to do is start doing some little something. Whether it is to benefit your health, benefit your marriage, or to benefit your business or your career.

You can eat the first apple of the new apple a day philosophy along with some other things you have decided to do. You could say one of these days I will never be healed again. I'm going to have all the breath I need. I'm going to have all the vitality I need. I'm munching on the first apple.

You don't have to revolutionize all at once. Just start.

But, the first apple you eat, if it's a plan to better health, I'm telling you, by the end of that first day your self-esteem starts to grow.

Say to yourself, "I promise myself I'll never be the same again."

It doesn't take a revolution. You don't have to do spectacularly dramatic things for self-esteem to start going off the scale. Just make a commitment to any easy discipline. Then another one and another one.

It doesn't take but just a collection of those new easy disciplines to start giving you the idea that you're going to change every part of your life: financial, spiritual, social.

A year from now, you'll be almost unrecognizable as the mediocre person you may have been up until now. All of that can change.

It doesn't change overnight. But, it does change with a change in thought and philosophy. Pick up a new discipline and start it immediately.

Litman
When you bring up action, like Jack Canfield on the show a while ago talking about the universe rewards action, we talked about the concept of doing it

personally. We can both concur on this, amazing things happen.

Those little baby steps create momentum. They create energy, force, and they create something that I want to steer back to.

You talk a lot about ambition, the fuel of achievement. You talk about being ambitious.

I personally saw my life revolutionized when I found something that I enjoyed and made it a necessity to be ambitious about it.

Talk about the power of ambition. How do we build a life where we become ambitious?

Rohn

Sometimes ambition just lingers below the surface. All of the possibilities for ambition are there.

But, if you live an undisciplined life drifting on health, drifting on relationships, drifting on developing a better career, if you're drifting, it doesn't taste good at the end of the day. But, if you start something, I promise you, not only will you feel better about yourself in terms of self esteem, which develops self confidence, which is one of the greatest things in stepping towards success, it'll also start awakening a spark of ambition.

A person who has never sold anything in their life. Finally they get a product they can believe in. They make the first sale and all of a sudden they say, "Gosh, if I did this once, I can do it again."

By the time they've made the tenth sale they say, "This could be the career for me. It could be the steps I need to become a leader. To become a giant in my field."

All of that stuff has the potential of awakening your ambition. To make the flames start to burn. It starts to grow.

But, it just doesn't grow unless you start the process.

You can't just say, "I'm praying and hoping that ambition will seize me tomorrow morning and everything will change."

Just start with some little something to prove to yourself that you're going to develop a whole list of disciplines.

Start with the easy ones first. It doesn't matter. Like making the necessary contacts in whatever business you're in.

If you make three phone calls a day, in a year that's a thousand.

Three does not sound like much. But, in a year it's a thousand.

If you make three positive calls a day, if you make a thousand positive calls, something phenomenal is going to happen to your life.

I also teach that the things that are easy to do are easy not to do.

If you want to learn a new language, three words a day, at the end of the year it gives you a vocabulary of a thousand words.

It's just easy to, but it's easy not to. It's easier to hope it will get better than to start the process of making it better.

That is really the theme of my seminars.

Litman
(To Listeners)

On the topic of seminars, go to jimrohn.com to find out more about Jim's seminars. When you go to jimrohn.com subscribe to his newsletter.

There are tons of people that Jim has influenced and you'll hear the information tonight.

(Back to Jim)

Talk about the power, simplicity, and importance of having strong reasons.

Rohn

That's major. If you have enough reasons, you can do anything.

If you have enough reasons, you'll read all the books you need to read.

If you have enough reasons, enough goals, enough objectives, enough things that you want to accomplish in your life, you'll attend whatever classes you need to attend. You'll get up however early you need to get up.

Sometimes we find it a little hard to get out of bed. We want to linger. Part of that is not just being tired, or weary, or a little bit of poor nutrition, some of it is just lack of the drive in terms of having a long enough list of reasons to do it.

Then you've just got to let the reasons grow. Things you thought were important this year, you go for them, then next year you look back and you say, "I was a little foolish about that. Here's what I really want. That isn't really important to me anymore." Then you just keep up this process of what's important to you.

For your family, build a financial wall around your family nothing can get through. I made that statement, about six years ago, to a young couple that has twins. Fabulous. They now earn about five to six million dollars a year.

I remember the day they came to me and said, "You know that statement you made about building a financial wall around your family that nothing can get through? Well, we resolved to do that. Now we're happy to report to you that we have just crossed the line. We have now finished building the financial wall around our family nothing can get through."

I'm telling you, the power of something like that is amazing. That's just a small example of all the things that can inspire your life.

Where do you want to go? Who do you want to meet? How many skills do you want to learn this year? How many languages do you want to learn?

I go and lecture in the Scandinavian countries. They all speak four or five, six languages.

In the school system you are required to learn four languages. Three they assign, and one you can pick.

I mean, there isn't anything you can't do in terms of language, skills, business, financial independence, or being a person of benevolence.

The famous story of Latorno, back when I was a kid, was an inspiring story. He finally got to the place where he could give away 90% of his income.

My mentor, Mr. Shoaff, knew the story and said to me, "Wouldn't that be great for you, Mr. Rohn? To finally get to the place where you could give away 90%?" I thought, "Wow that would be incredible."

Somebody says, "90%. Wow that's a lot to give away." Well, you should have seen the 10% that was left. It was not peanuts.

But anyway, those kinds of dreams, those kinds of goals are what really start the fire. At first you just need the goals that start triggering activity immediately.

Say, "I want to be able to pay my rent on time within 90 days. I'm putting in a little extra time. I'm doing this, I'm doing that. I'm taking the class. Whatever. After 90 days, I'm never going to be late on my rent again. I'm tired of the creditors calling. What are my goals?"

I heard a knock on my door back when I was about 24. I went to the door and there was a Girl Scout selling cookies. She gives me the big pitch. Girl Scouts, best organization in the world, we've got this variety of cookies, just $2.00. Then, with a big smile, she asked me to buy.

I wanted to buy. That wasn't a problem. Big problem, though, was I didn't have $2.00 in my pocket.

I was a grown man. I had a family. A couple of kids. I had been to college one year. I didn't have $2.00 in my pocket.

I didn't want to tell her I was that broke. So, I lied to her and said, "Hey, I've already bought lots of Girl Scout cookies. Still got plenty in the house."

So, she said, "Well, that's wonderful. Thank you very much," and she left.

When she left, I said to myself "I don't want to live like this anymore. How low can you get? Lying to a Girl Scout. I mean, that's about as low as you can go."

So, that became an obsession for me.

From that day on I said, "I'm immediately going to acquire whatever it takes to have a pocket full of money so that no matter where I am for the rest of my life, no matter how many Girl Scouts are there, no matter how many cookies they've got to sell, I'll be able to buy them all."

It just triggered something.

Now, that's not a ranch in Montana. That's not becoming a billionaire. But, it was enough of an incentive to get me started.

Shoaff taught me that you have to carry money in your pocket. He said,

"Five hundred dollars in your pocket feels better than $500 in the bank."

I couldn't wait 'til the moment when I had $500 in my pocket.

It doesn't take much to get started. Then the list goes on from there.

Then if you have enough of those reasons, don't tell me you won't get up early, stay up late, read the book, listen to the cassette, do the deal, take notes, keep a journal, work on your language, or work on your skills.

I'm telling you, it's all wrapped up there: dreams, visions, setting goals, starting with something simple.

Litman

When you talk about reasons, Jim, don't many of those strong reasons come out of a pain in one's life?

Rohn

Sure.

Litman

Okay. Because I know from my own life that it can come from necessity and it can come out of pain and trying to get away from that.

Rohn

The pain of not having $2.00 was pain enough.

Nobody else witnessed it, but me and the Girl Scout. Of course, I'm sure she didn't notice it because she accepted my lie and moved on.

But, I said, "I don't want this to happen anymore."

It was such an incredible resolve and it was only over $2.00. But it doesn't matter what it is.

If it's something you want to correct, something you never want to happen again, that's the beginning.

Litman

You're well known internationally about the power of goals, the key formula for success.

Can you tell us about goals? The importance of goals, but more specifically, how do you set them?

Do you think them? Do you write them down? Can you walk us through the power and the process of goal setting?

Rohn

In my two-day leadership seminar, I go through a little workshop. It's called Designing The Next Ten Years.

It's really a simple process.

Start making lists of what you want.

I teach the simple, simple ways. Others have got some complicated ways of setting goals and deadlines and all that stuff. I don't do that.

I just say to make a list of the books you want to read. Make a list of the places you want to go. Start making a list of the things you wish to acquire.

What kind of education do you want for your family? Make a list. Where are the place you want to visit? Make a list.

What kind of experiences do you want to have? Make a list.

Decide what you want. Then write it all down. Put a lot of little things on there so you can start checking some things off. Because part of the fun of having the list is checking it off. No matter how small it is.

My first list had a little revenge. Some of the people who said I couldn't do well. They went on my list. I couldn't wait to get my new car and drive it up on their lawn. A few little things on revenge.

It doesn't matter what it is. It's your personal list. You can tear it up and throw it away if you want and then get started on it.

Later you can say as you look back, "I was all hot on this idea. Now, here's something I know that is much better. I'm going to forget about that other thing." So, it's an ongoing, continual process.

But, I have discovered that if you think about the things you want for you, your family, some goals are individual, some are collective, some are family, some are business, just start with that. Rearrange it any way you want to. You don't have to have any deadlines. You can look at the list after you've made it and start putting a 1, 3, 5 or 10 number beside each item. You know, "I think I can accomplish that in about a year. I think I can accomplish that in about three years. I think I can accomplish that in about five years." Something like that. But, it's easy.

Success is easy. Especially in America it's easy. Bangladesh, it's hard. Cambodia, it's hard. America, it's easy.

If you don't believe that, if you think easy is hard, then you are in trouble all your life.

We've got to teach our kids. Some of them have the concept that America is hard. They don't understand the difference between Bangladesh and America.

The average income in Bangladesh is about $100 a year. That's what's hard.

If you understand what's hard and what's easy, you can say, "Wow, it ought to be easy here."

The only reason for not doing well here, is not applying yourself for some information to learn, and then start to practice right away.

You've got to practice. You have to do the deal. You read this book on good health, right?

It talks about nutrition and it talks about exercise then in the middle of the book the author says, "Now reader, set this book aside. Fall on the floor and see how many push-ups you can do." Then, of course, you don't do that. So, you read on and the author says, "If you didn't set this book aside and if you didn't fall on the floor to see how many push-ups you can do, why don't you just give this book away? Why bother yourself with reading if you're not going to pick an idea and try it?"

That's such great advice.

Litman

Ok, I want to bring something up and see if you agree with me on it.

We're talking about taking action. We're talking about planning, ambition, and taking those baby steps.

It seems to me, in my own personal life, when you start taking the steps, start changing your thinking, start moving forward toward a dream or vision, it almost seems like the universe conspires with you to help you. Do you see that as well?

Rohn

Absolutely!

A phrase in the Bible seems to indicate that whatever you move towards, moves towards you.

It mentions that God said, "If you make a move toward me, I'll make a move toward you."

If you move toward education, it seems like the possibilities of education start moving your way.

If you move toward good health, the ideas for better health, the information starts moving toward you.

That's good advice.

If you'll just start the process of moving toward what you want, it is true, mysteriously, by some unique process, life loves to reward its benefactors.

If you start taking care of something, it wants to reward you by producing and looking well.

If you take care of flowers, they seem to bloom especially for you and say, "Look how pretty we are. You have taken such good care of us. Now we want to give back to you by giving you our beauty."

I taught my two girls how to swim and dive. Of course, like all kids, they'd say, "Daddy, watch me. Watch me do this dive." It's almost like they're saying, 'You're the one that taught me. You're the one that had patience with me. You invested part of your life in this process. Now watch me. Watch how good I am."

All of life wishes to do that. All life wishes to reward its benefactor.

It could be something like a garden that grows because you took the time to cultivate it, to pull out the weeds, and take care of the bugs. Now, the garden does extremely well for you as a reflection back to you Because you are the one that invested time, energy, effort, and a piece of your life.

Litman

Let's stay here, Jim. Talk about the power of giving and the word "tithing." Can we talk about giving and what happens when someone gives?

Rohn

I teach a little formula for kids called seventy, ten, ten, and ten.

This formula is about never spending more than 70 cents out of every dollar you earn.

The way it works is that ten cents is for active capital, ten cents is for passive capital, and then ten cents is to give away.

Whether it's to your church, a benevolent organization, or whether you let someone else manage it, or you manage it yourself.

We've got to teach generosity right from the beginning. I teach that ten percent is a good figure to start with.

You know when you become rich and wealthy, it can be 20, 30, 40, 50, 60, 70, 80, 90.

Whatever.

But, ten cents is the start.

If you teach generosity, I'm telling you, kids will give you a dime out of every dollar to help someone that can't help themselves.

It's about what it does for you spiritually. Do it for what it brings back to you in terms of self-esteem.

Help to enrich the world by giving, and not only 10 percent of your money, but maybe some percentage of your time as well.

That investment is a smart investment.

It may bring returns to you immediately in ways you don't even know. It can do amazing things for your character, your reputation, and your inner spirit. It's all worth it!

Someone might say, "Well, I gave to this organization and they misused it."

It doesn't matter to you whether they misused it or not. The key for you is that you gave. They've got to be responsible on their own side.

No matter what though, giving is a major piece. Then, the next step is giving somebody your ideas.

This mentor I met when I was 25, Earl Shoaff, is someone I have to thank for the rest of my life for taking the time to share with me a bit of his philosophy that revolutionized my life.

I was never the same again after the first year. No one has ever had to say to me after the first year I was with him, "When are you going to get going? When are you going to get off the dime?"

I've never heard that since that first year that I met this man who gave me his ideas and he did it freely.

He did it with great excitement. Because he knew that if he invested in me, I would probably invest in someone else.

Sure enough, that turned out to be true.

Litman

Ok. It's been 38 years or so. You're entering your second decade of doing this.

Where does the continuous passion and inspiration come from for you? Why are you still doing this?

Rohn

It's very exciting because it's made me several fortunes and continues to do so.

But, part of the greatest excitement is when your name appears in somebody's testimonial.

You know, someone says something like, "I was at a certain place in my life and I listened to this person and it changed my life."

Mark Hughes, the founder of HerbaLife, used to say that because he attended my seminar when he was 19 it changed his life. He said, "I attended Jim Rohn's seminar and he was the first person that gave me the idea that in spite of my background I could make changes and become successful."

You can imagine how that made me feel. It's amazing for me to have my name appearing in his testimonial.

But, whether it's Mark Hughes or someone else, it doesn't matter.

Imagine this scenario: You've got someone who says, "Let me introduce you to the person that changed my life five years ago. We were sitting at Denny's five years ago and he recommended this book to me. He told me that it has really helped him. So, he recommended it to me. Well, as I look back on it now, that was the beginning of some incredible life changes for me. Look where I am today. I'm telling you, it started five years ago at Denny's on a Tuesday morning when this person introduced me to this book."

So, you don't have to give seminars. You don't have to give lectures. You don't even have to write books to affect someone's life and to do it so well that your name appears in their testimonial some day.

You know, someone says, "Here's the person who believed in me until I could believe in myself. Someone who saw more in me than I could see at the beginning."

Litman

Let's stay here, Jim. Because there's something I want to get across to people. It's such a powerful statement that you talk about. I've heard you talk about the concept of, sure, we want to reach our destination. We want to reach our goals. But, more importantly, Jim, can you talk about the power in the being and the becoming?

Rohn

Well, true. What we acquire of course is valuable. But, the greatest value is not what we acquire. The greatest value is what we become.

My mentor had an interesting way of teaching it. When I was 25 years old he said, "I suggest, Mr. Rohn, that you set a goal to become a millionaire."

I was all intrigued by that. You know, it's got a nice ring to it—millionaire.

Then he said, "Here's why…" I thought to myself, "Gosh, he doesn't need to teach me why. Wouldn't it be great to have a million dollars?" Then he said, "No then you'll never acquire it.

Here's why. Set a goal to become a millionaire for what it makes of you to achieve it."

Litman

Can you say that again please?

Rohn

"Set a goal to become a millionaire for what it makes of you to achieve it."

He said, "Do it for the skills you have to learn and the person you have to become. Do it for what you'll end up knowing about the marketplace, what you'll learn about the management of time and working with people. Do it for the ability of discovering how to keep your ego in check. For what you have to learn about being benevolent. Being kind as well as being strong. What you have to learn about society and business and government and taxes and becoming an accomplished person to reach the status of millionaire.

All that you have learned and all that you've become to reach the status of millionaire is what's valuable. Not the million dollars.

If you do it that way, then once you become a millionaire, you can give all the money away.

Because it's not the money that's really important. What's important is the person you have become."

That was one of the best pieces of philosophy I have ever heard in my life. Nobody ever shared it with me like that before.

Another thing he said was, "Beware of what you become in pursuit of what you want. Don't sell out. Don't sell out your principles. Don't compromise your values. Because you might acquire something by doing so, but it won't taste good."

An old prophet said, "Sometimes what tastes good in the mouth finally turns bitter in the belly." Then, later we regret that we compromised or that we did something incredibly wrong to acquire something. It's not worth it. If we do that, then what we get is worthless.

If you use something like that to challenge yourself to grow, to reach a certain level, I think it's wise. Because then you know where the true value is and that is in the person you become.

Litman

I want to reverse back to about 90 seconds ago when you were talking about your great mentor, Earl Nightingale. You talked about the ability to express gratitude. To express thanks.

I feel, in my own life, an aspect of gratitude is very important.

So, number one, do you agree with that, and two, can you talk about the power of that word—gratitude?

Rohn

Well, it absolutely is very important.

I made a little list the other day as I reminisced about the things that really made such an incredible contribution to my life.

Number one on my list, of course, was my parents.

I was an only child. They spoiled me. They laid a foundation for me that has kept me steady all these years.

The more I thought about it, I thought, "What a contribution they've made to my life.'

A lot of it, at the moment, I couldn't see. I didn't realize. But, as the years began to unfold, I realized that what they taught me, the care they gave me, the love they shared with me, that no matter what happened to me, I always had a place I could always go home to.

They provided that kind of unique stability.

They didn't just say, 'Son, you can do it." It was also the advice they gave me and the prayers they sent me, no matter where I went around the world, because I believe in that, the power of prayer.

Every once in awhile I get a letter and someone says, "Mr. Rohn, we are praying for you." I read it and think, "Wow. This is some kind of letter when someone takes the time to say a prayer."

My gratitude for that is just unending.

Litman

Talk about the power of prayer.

Rohn

Who knows, you know, the mystery of prayer and God.

In the Declaration of Independence it says, we are created equal. But it says also that, we are endowed by our Creator with gifts and rights.

It's a philosophy America believes in that we are a special creation. That we have these gifts based on a Creator.

We open the Senate with prayer. We put on our money "In God We Trust." We are that kind of nation really.

When I travel the world, people ask me, "How come America does so well?" I say, "Read the money." I think that is probably part of it. That kind of trust, that kind of In God We Trust, implies prayer and I think that it is so vital.

It doesn't have to be in a church, synagogue, mosque, or anywhere else. It doesn't have to be in a formal place. But, I think it's a tremendous power.

Litman

We're talking about the power of thankfulness, of gratitude.

Jim, I want to put on my world-famous, internationally renowned, two-minute warning with you.

All that means is we have about ten minutes left to rock 'n roll, and shake and bake.

Let's talk about the best-kept secret of the rich, time management. Tell me about the importance of it and how we become effective time managers.

Rohn

Well, first is to realize how precious time is.

There's not an unending supply of years in your life.

My father lived to be 93 and it still seemed very short. I kept asking for another ten years, another ten years, another five years.

Surely, Papa can live to be 100, I'd think.

I'd love to have him see the 21st Century, which was not to be. But, 93 years still seems short.

The Beatles wrote, "Life is very short." For John Lennon it was extra short. There is not an unending supply of the days and the moments.

The key is to utilize them to the best of your ability. Don't just let them slip away.

Capture them, like we capture the seasons. There is only so many.

In ninety years you have ninety spring times. If some guy says, you know, "I got twenty more years." You say, "No. You got twenty more times."

If you go fishing once a year you only have twenty more times to go fishing. Now that starts to make it a bit more critical. Not that I have a whole twenty more years, but just twenty more times. How valuable do I want to make these twenty times?

It doesn't matter whether it's going to the concert or sitting down with your family, or taking a vacation. There is only so many.

It's easy not to plan and do the details necessary to make them the best possible.

Then I have other little ideas like, "Don't start the day, until you have it finished."

Litman

Say that again, Jim.

Rohn

Don't start the day until you have it finished.

It's a key for executives, a key for leadership. But it's also a key for a mother at home. It doesn't matter, whoever.

Plan the day to the best of your abilities.

There will be plenty of room for surprises and innovations and whatever. Give a good plan, a good schedule for the day.

Because each day is a piece of the mosaic of your life.

You can either just cross your fingers and say, "I hope it will work out okay," or you can give it some attention and say, "Here's what I would like to accomplish in the next twenty-four hours."

Just look at it that way and do a lot of it up front or maybe the night before. Start the day after you finished it.

It's like building a house. If I asked you, "When should you start building the house that you want to build?" and you say to me, "Well, that's a good question. When should I start building the house?" I've got an excellent answer for you. The answer is, you start building it as soon as you have it finished.

You know, someone might say, "Is it possible to finish a house before you start it?" The answer is, yes. It would be foolish to start it until you had it finished.

Imagine if you just started laying bricks. Somebody could come by and ask, "What are you building here?" You say, "I have no idea. I'm just laying bricks and well see how it works out." They would call you foolish and maybe take you away to a safe place.

The key is that it's possible to finish a day before you start it. It's possible to finish a month before you start it.

I do business around the world with colleagues in about 50 countries. To do business around the world in 50 countries you can't imagine all of the preparatory planning that has to be done. Some things are three years, five years, two years, one year ahead in order to do that kind of global business.

But, if you just learned to be disciplined enough to start with the day plan, the month plan, your good health plan, I'm telling you, you will take advantage of time like you can't believe.

Litman

Jim, let's bring up a few topics and go 30 to 45 seconds on each, if we can.

You're one of the most effective communicators of the last 50 years or so. You've talked in front of 4 million people and you've influenced millions beyond that through your books and tapes.

What's the most important communication tip you can give us right now?

Rohn

You just need a desire to be a great communicator and keep improving the art every day. It's easy to be careless with your language in social areas, but that's going to affect your business.

You just have to start practicing the art of better language, whether it's social, personal, home, or family.

You can't say, "Oh, it's with my family, so my language doesn't really matter." It really does matter because it's so valuable for them. But, also because it's so valuable for you to practice the art.

It's like this telephone conversation. If I thought, "Well, I don't have 35,000 people to talk to. So, I'll treat this conversation carelessly." I just learn not to do that.

I want to give the most concise and best information I can, even though it's a telephone conversation and not a big audience in some auditorium.

Litman

So, we're talking here about being on purpose, about changing language, changing your mindset.

When a person goes for something, there are roadblocks to steer away from. There are adversities. Talk about the power of resilience.

Rohn

You've just got to be able to come back. Come back from a disappointment. It takes a bit of courage.

If you start a sales career and the first person you approach says, "No", you've got to have the courage to talk to the second person.

If you start a little business, set up the first meeting, and nobody joins, you've got to have the courage to say, "I'll set up another meeting. Because if one person says no it doesn't mean everybody's going to say no."

You've just got to have that ability to come back.

You've got to understand the law of averages. Not everybody is going to be interested in your project. Not everybody is going to buy your product.

You can't take it personally.

Then, if you get hit by poor health, you've just got to do everything within your power to get well.

If you face a disappointment, you've got to come back. From a divorce, you've got to come back. It's going to hurt for a while, you've got to let it linger and do whatever it's going to do. But, then you've got to build back.

That's part of the game of life.

It's no different for you, me, or anyone else.

Resilience, we all need it. Whether it's health, marriage, family, business, social, or personal.

Litman
Talk about the power of enlightened self-interest.

Rohn
Yes, life doesn't give us what we need. Life gives us what we deserve.

If you want wealth, it's okay to wish for wealth if you pay the proper price for wealth.

Litman
So, there is a price to be paid.

Rohn
You can pay the proper price without diminishing anyone else. Once I learned that, I got excited about being wealthy in my own self-interest. Everybody wins.

Litman

What we're talking about here is coming from a position of integrity and creating wealth for the benefit of others.

I ask this question to a lot of the people, Mark Victor Hansen, Robert Allen, and a lot of the people I have interviewed. I always thought it was a melancholy question, but they have told me it isn't.

We're all going to pass on some day. What do you want the world to say about Jim Rohn when that day does come?

Rohn

That he invested his life wisely and as best he could to help as many people to change their lives as possible and that he blessed his own life. That's really it.

Litman

You talk about self-education. You talk about how it's the seed of fortune. Are there any books out there, in addition to your own at jimrohn.com, that you can recommend to my audience?

Rohn

Well, sure. Shoaff recommended *Think and Grow Rich* to me when I first started learning.

Litman

What was the most powerful thing you took out of Think and Grow Rich?

Rohn

Desire, determination, preset plans, never give up, persistence, it's got a wealth of information in it.

Litman

Anything else come to mind?

Rohn

The Richest Man in Babylon helped me to become a millionaire by age 32. Simple little book. Easy-to-follow. Inspiring. *The Richest Man in Babylon*, by George Clauson.

Litman

Jim, we're wrapping down the show tonight. Jim, it's been an absolute gold-mine and a pleasure to share you with my audience. Jim Rohn, thank you very much for appearing on The Mike Litman Show.

Rohn

It's been a pleasure, Mike. We'll do it again sometime.

About Jim Rohn

For more than 40 years, Jim Rohn honed his craft like a skilled artist—helping people the world over sculpt life strategies that have expanded their imagination of what is possible. Jim authored countless books and audio and video programs, and helped motivate and shape an entire generation of personal-development trainers and hundreds of executives from America's top corporations.

At 25, he met his mentor, Earl Shoaff. And over the next six years he made his first fortune, yet didn't get into speaking until he moved to Beverly Hills, California, when a friend at the Rotary Club asked him to tell his success story, which Rohn titled "Idaho Farm Boy Makes It to Beverly Hills."

His speech went over so well that he received more invitations to share it, and better yet, they started paying him for it. In the beginning, he spoke in front of college and high-school classes and at service clubs, before moving on to seminars in 1963, which launched him into the personal-development business. From then on, Jim Rohn became a trailblazer in the self-help and personal development industry, impacting the lives of millions through his life-changing material.

Jim is known as one of the great wordsmiths of our time. Here is a sampling from Jim's *Treasury of Quotes* that reflect on his philosophy on life and business:

Skills: Don't wish it were easier; wish you were better. Don't wish for less problems; wish for more skills. Don't wish for less challenges; wish for more wisdom.

Growth: Don't join an easy crowd. You won't grow. Go where the expectations and the demands to perform and achieve are high.

Change: We generally change ourselves for one of two reasons: inspiration or desperation.

Jim shared his message with more than 6,000 audiences and over 5 million people all over the world. Jim's philosophies and influence continue to have worldwide impact.

Chapter 20

An Ordinary Guy with a Strong Enough Why

BY OZ KOREN

"If you work hard on the job, you will make a living,
If you work hard on yourself you will make a fortune."

- Jim Rohn

"Whether you think you can, or you think you can't—you're right." – A great quote by Henry Ford. It connects directly to the law of attraction. When teaching others about success, I like taking a more direct approach: "Stop saying 'I can't!' Instead, start asking 'How can I?'"

My name is Oz, I'm 35, a third-generation musician, married to my amazing wife, Tali, and the father of two boys, my pride and joy, Ofeq (4) and Ariel (almost 3). I left my last job just before Ofeq was born, and I've been blessed to lead an incredible lifestyle filled with travel, adventure, fun and joy. In fact, my wife and I just returned home to Israel from a nice vacation in Riviera Maya, Mexico. When we got back, we were tired from traveling, so we took the boys and went to relax at one of the nicest hotels by the Dead Sea. I'm not telling you this to impress you, but more to impress upon you that if I can do that, you CAN do that too!

Through the years, I've learned how to create several streams of passive income, which allows me to do whatever I want with my time. Just imagine! Today, I'm able to do what most people only dream of (as they sit stuck in traffic). Why? *Because I've devoted my life to learning how to do it.* What's more, I had the courage to execute what I learned—even when it meant failing, as was often the case (especially when I was trying something new).

Also, I learned very early that, to get what I wanted, I would have to overcome the obstacles.

Since I was a little boy, starting probably around the age of three, I had an understanding of this concept. In fact, one of my earliest childhood memories centers on this very thing. I was at daycare; it was after lunch, and all the little kids were taking their afternoon nap. I, being a very active kid, didn't need to take a nap. In fact, even now I never take naps because there's always so much to do. Anyway, everyone was taking a nap that day, and the teacher was using the time to mop the floor. I remember needing to go to the restroom, but she yelled at me for getting off my mat and wouldn't let me go. The next few days during naptime, she wouldn't let me play around or do anything else except sit on my mat. That was when I knew I had to figure something out. I was *not* just going to sit there for two hours every day. So after getting my parents on board, we decided that during naptime I would go to older kids' classroom to play with them. That way, everybody was happy. That's just the first of many similar situations throughout my life where, instead of accepting someone's "no," I simply figured out a way around it.

It's not that I'm all that smart or talented, but I *am* a fast learner and a very hard worker. I also discovered early on that most people around me were a bit lazy. So by spending just a little more time learning what I needed to, I could always get ahead. I also realized that I could get what I wanted *if* I wanted it badly enough.

The first time that I remember that strong motivation inside of me really impacting my life dramatically was when I tried out for a special high school for musicians. My grandfather had played with an orchestra in Germany before World War II, and my father was a musician for many years, playing at clubs and weddings, etc. However, never having been classically trained himself, that's what he wanted for me—and I was. But, because I didn't start early enough, I always had to work harder than those around me. The first time I really "got it" about how desire and motivation can make the deciding difference was when I wanted to get into this high school. I had an audition, but I was rejected outright; they told me to work extra hard and come back the following year. Several months later I wanted to go to a different school, so I auditioned there. Again, I was told no. I was only fifteen, and the double blow devastated me. But instead of giving up, I wrote the school and asked for another chance—I asked to take another audition and more tests. I guess someone there must have been impressed with my spunk, because they let me proceed to the next admission stages. I did my absolute best once again and, finally, they said yes!

Even though I started that school as one of its worst pupils, I was a teacher's dream: working as hard as anyone else—and even harder. Be fore I knew it, I had finished the first of three years of high school with very good grades and a growing musical talent. Now that's a funny word, "talent." Talent is when you're terrible at first, but you keep working at it for ten years. Suddenly, people who haven't been around you in a while see what you've accomplished, and voilà—you've got talent!

Of course, if you're practicing something for six hours or more every day, that "talent" is going to come even sooner than ten years. My musical career continued from high school through college in the U.S. I got my Bachelor's degree in classical saxophone and then my Master's degree in orchestral conducting. I won many scholarships and competitions, and was living my dream of becoming a professional musician.

Back home after college, I played with the Israeli Philharmonic and performed throughout Israel. But then the disaster of 9/11 happened, and there was not much left of my musical career. I guess people were on edge during those scary and uncertain times and didn't feel like getting out to listen to classical music that much. After several months of calling, waiting and hoping, I had to get a J.O.B. (Just Over Broke). So I started working as a gym instructor, because of the flexibility it afforded of allowing me to work in shifts, in case I would get a call to perform somewhere. However, after more than two years of being broke and living like a starving artist, it became apparent that it was time to get a "real job."

One of my gym clients got me an interview for a sales position with a real estate company. I was offered the job and eagerly accepted, not really knowing what I was getting into. Overworked and underpaid, I made only about $800 a month. After four months of no sales, my manager was very upset, basically letting me know in no uncertain terms that I had no chance of succeeding in real estate and that I should go back to music.

I, however, saw things differently. I had a strong motivation (mainly the need for food and a place to live!), and so I got my real estate broker's license and started working as a real estate agent for a different company. That was the hardest job I ever had, but through it I met a lot of rich people and started learning about real estate investing. I read *Rich Dad, Poor Dad* and learned for the first time about the concept of residual income. Several months later, I combined all my savings and took out a loan to purchase my first piece of real estate. Today, seven years later, I own several units free and clear, and I'm happy to say they are generating a nice residual income for my family and me.

Before Tali and I were married, when I was looking for a different job (one that actually pays), she arranged for me to interview with an advanced technologies company for a sales position. Despite having no technical background or experience in that field whatsoever, I was determined to get that job. I went to three interviews and pretty much failed each one of them miserably. But the CEO of the company, who had no other candidates and/or must have appreciated my tenacity, decided to give me a chance. For over three months, all I did was come into the office and just learn. I learned about the technology, the equipment, the competition—everything. Eventually, I went out into the field to start selling.

But I didn't sell anything. In fact, for about seven months I didn't sell one system, which naturally made my boss and the CEO pretty nervous. But finally I made my first sale, and then another one, and another. I ended up selling about $250,000 worth of equipment my first year. By the next year I had honed my skills even further, selling more than $500,000 that year. By my third year, I brought the account to about $1.3 million in revenue. In addition, I was managing several other people who were also making sales. Looking back on those three years, I realize that my growth didn't just happen by chance. It was a direct result of all the effort I'd put toward the goal of learning everything I could about the company, the product and what set it apart from the competition.

Not long after I started working there, I was introduced to the concept of network marketing, or multilevel marketing. Once again, I had no idea what it was all about, but I was fascinated by the concept and decided I was going to do it. My first three months in the MLM business were terrible. I signed up only two people, one of them was my sister, and I paid for her initial order!

But one of the most wonderful things about the network marketing industry is that you must embrace personal development to experience success. So that is precisely what I did. I learned all I could about success, communication and leadership—and I learned it from people who had achieved real results, not just some college professor with theories only. I immersed myself in personal development and financial education. I read a lot of books, listened to hundreds of tapes and CDs and spent a great deal of money on seminars and events, all of which helped me build a huge business within several years. Even now, I invest time every day learning and practicing personal development.

As Jim Rohn said, "I was working on my job to make a living, but I was working on *myself* to make a fortune!" As I applied everything I was learning to all aspects of my life, the results were amazing. I started selling much more, thus earning much more money at my job, *and* my network marketing business grew!

At this point in my success, I made a critical decision that served me very well. I wisely kept my lifestyle at a moderately comfortable level, investing the money that I was saving to buy more real estate and create more sources of residual income. I've known many who have given in to the temptation to increase their lifestyle spending as soon as they started making more money, rather than using that income to reinvest and fuel more growth. I always wonder why they would want to cut themselves short of their full potential.

About four years ago, I "won" the rat race. I'm now able to work on my various businesses from home, or anywhere else in the world for that matter. Many people say I have the Midas Touch, but they don't know how many times I failed or how hard I worked to get what I wanted. The way I see it, the secret to success is first to have big dreams—to know *what* you want but, more importantly, *why* you want it. Second, you have to take immediate and massive action following a detailed plan for achieving those goals and dreams. And third, never let anyone tell you: "*You can't!*" especially not yourself.

About Oz Koren

Oz Koren is a gifted musician and an entrepreneur. Oz holds a Bachelor's degree in saxophone performance and a Master's degree in orchestral conducting. He studied with some of the best music professors in the world, won many awards and scholarships, and played concerts and recitals all over the U.S. and Israel, including performances with the Israeli Philharmonic.

In 2005, he shifted careers and took a position as a marketing and sales manager, selling advanced technologies. During the same year he began investing in real estate and in the stock market. That shift was a direct result of following the path of personal development and self improvement. Today, in addition to expanding his various businesses, he is focused on helping thousands of people get out of the "rat race" by owning their own businesses and taking control of their lives.